The Emergence of LEISURE

Basic Conditions of Life

The Emergence of LEISURE

Edited with an Introduction by
MICHAEL R. MARRUS

HARPER TORCHBOOKS
Harper & Row, Publishers
New York, Evanston, San Francisco, London

Contents

Introduction

Can there be a history of leisure? Clearly, historians have not devoted a great deal of attention to this subject, and students will have difficulty uncovering much material about it. For leisure does not really seem "serious." One sociologist goes even further and claims that many people are uncomfortable when discussing leisure: "as with sex, they want to make a joke about it."[1] If this is in fact a common reaction among scholars in general and historians in particular, there are grounds for believing that the topic is more important than sometimes allowed. For whenever such uncommon sensitivity is perceived, the amateur psychologist in each of us is usually suspicious. Considering the matter more closely, we may be able to discover some things

1. David Riesman, *Individualism Reconsidered and Other Essays* (Glencoe, Illinois: The Free Press, 1954), p. 202.

about our own attitudes to leisure which we did not fully understand before. Leisure may well turn out to be important.

Historians have not been alone in their failure to delve into this problem. Surveying the field of social thought since the Protestant Reformation, scholars have been hard pressed to distinguish the landmarks of this particular theme. Scattered indications, however, have been identified. During the sixteenth and seventeenth centuries the French writers Montaigne and Pascal had some things to say about the role of diversion in life; differing on almost every issue, they were at odds on this question too. Montaigne, the earlier of the two, believed in the beneficial effects of escapist activity in the face of human pain and suffering, while Pascal feared the corrupting effects on man's quest for salvation. Montaigne was inclined to smile warmly upon man in his search for amusement, while Pascal was deeply suspicious. Their differences, expressed in various ways, have echoed in the writings of their successors even up to our own times. During the eighteenth century a small army of moralists strenuously campaigned on behalf of another point of view—that leisure be put to good effect. For time, as Benjamin Franklin solemnly said, was money, and "he that can earn ten shillings a day by labor, and goes abroad or sits idle one half of that day, though he spends but sixpence during his diversion and idleness, ought not to reckon that the only expense; he has really spent, or rather thrown away, five shillings besides." Concealed in this genial homily was another attitude to leisure which is familiar in our own day: leisure was a wasteful drain on productive enterprise. It was precisely this kind of stern injunction which socialists in the nineteenth century attacked so bitterly. Karl Marx's son-in-law, Paul Lafargue, was one of these critics who addressed the question of leisure. Writing in 1883, Lafargue proclaimed for the working class "the right to be lazy," to be won through a liberation from the brutally intensified work rhythms of modern capitalism.

Now common to all of these perspectives, over the course of several centuries, is the notion that leisure must always be judged in relation to something else—the anguish of human existence according to Montaigne, the perilous search for spiritual perfection according to Pascal, the earnest commitment to work according to Franklin, and the mechanisms of capitalist exploitation according to Lafargue. None of these writers considered leisure on its own terms; none of them thought about it except in relation to some higher or more important purpose in life.

So long as leisure was seen in this fashion, as the negative complement of work or as the instrument of some larger enterprise, it could scarcely be considered "serious" in itself. In our own century, however, two developments have brought about a new focus. First, there is the emergence of a powerful school of social criticism both before and after the Second World War which fastened upon "popular culture" and mass leisure activities as one of the most important ingredients of the modern age. The Dutch historian Johan Huizinga, the Spanish philosopher Ortega y Gasset, and the American critic Clement Greenberg were all concerned with this theme; significantly, each had a sense that modern leisure forms were principal contributors to a debasement of the cultural values of Western civilization. In contrast with the brooding pessimism of these writers there is a second school of thought which derives from a slightly later period. Working in relative economic prosperity, a number of social scientists have speculated on the "society of leisure" which they argue is upon us. In this view the freeing of Western man from the cruel grip of necessity—in effect the need to work in order to obtain a meager subsistence—is one of the most significant changes in recorded history. Looking forward to a time when the amount of leisure at the disposal of the average person will enormously increase, they have begun to consider leisure as a challenge to social engineers who will contribute to the realization of the good life.[2] Usually, these differing perspectives oppose each other in their evaluation of leisure; while the former stands with Pascal, considering it a debasement, the latter tends to be much more optimistic, looking to a progressive improvement of the overall quality of leisure. But these value judgments are not as interesting to us here as the information upon which they are based. From our standpoint the important thing about each of these approaches is that they have inspired a scholarly consideration of leisure on its own terms. Until very recently, however, such work was limited to the fields of sociology and anthropology. Generally speaking, the interests of historians have tended to respond more sluggishly to contemporary

2. See, for example, Joffre Dumazedier, *Toward a Society of Leisure,* trans. Stewart E. McClure (New York: The Free Press, 1967).

concerns. There are signs now that this is changing, and the series of which this book is a part testifies to this.

Before going further, we might pause momentarily for definitions. Once leisure is judged worthy of attention in its own right we can identify it with greater precision, and in doing so a good deal of baggage which encumbered the common sense view of leisure begins to fall away. If leisure, for example, is no longer considered to be simply the negative complement of work, it cannot be seen as everything which is done outside the time spent working. Nor can it be confused with mere "recreation," this being sometimes at least associated with the kind of refreshment necessarily accompanying labor. But what, then, is leisure? Is it to include the entire array of sociocultural activities that men have engaged in exclusive of their work and other formal duties imposed by society? How is one to judge such various activities as visiting the family, playing games, puttering about the garden, taking a bath, going to church, hearing a lecture, and so on? Are these all leisure activities? Or only some? Several writers have cut through these problems in a manner, as we shall see, which makes sense in historical perspective. They have taken leisure to be that activity which occurs only in the absence of direct obligations—be they obligations of work, family, religion, or society. Leisure in this view is free activity which the individual engages in for his own purposes, whatever these may be. This leisure implies some degree of choice—a choice which may well be affected indirectly by social determinants but is made basically by autonomous individuals free from the long arm of traditional authority. In thus focusing on the element of choice they mean to draw a firm line between leisure and other kinds of nonwork activities which are deeply embedded in some form of group relationship. The latter activities may be enjoyable, joyous, symbolic, edifying, diverting, or instructive—as indeed work may be —but they are not leisure. No doubt, in this distinction there lurk all kinds of hidden philosophical pitfalls and problematic assumptions on such matters as the nature of freedom and the meaning of social determinism. But as a rough tool this notion can be useful. For the historian, moreover, it enables us to see more clearly that leisure has a history—a story of change and development. This is one conclusion to be drawn from this book.

The articles drawn together in this little volume tell a story—the emergence of leisure. At the center of it all is the argument that for the broad masses of Europeans, leisure became a reality only in the nineteenth century, and that its emergence was part of a more general transformation known as modernization.

In the beginning, as modern historians are sometimes wont to say, there was traditional society. Using this term scholars try to describe a package of institutions, beliefs, and relationships which stands in marked dissimilarity to those of our own society, which we think of as modern. Traditional society is usually taken to be that form of social life which prevailed in the Christian West from some time in the Middle Ages until some time in the eighteenth century. Traditional society was overwhelmingly rural, Christian, hierarchical, and ruled by custom. It was also often sick, cold, and hungry. Contemporary society, our present institutions, beliefs, and relationships, has emerged in the course of modernization, a powerful and sometimes traumatic process of social transformation which has been at work on various levels for several centuries. All of this, of course, is much too simple. But it does seem reasonable, in view of the general applicability of this scenario, to consider the unity of traditional social forms —not as a fixed or stable unity, but as a cluster of conditions which contrasts so dramatically with what was to follow.

According to the popular view of things, medieval rustics and most other common laborers in traditional society worked long hours of unremitting toil, and for the rest of their time lived bleak and monotonous lives. But historians know this popular view to be false. Rummaging about in the chronicles of daily life they have made rich discoveries of what seem to be leisure pursuits in traditional society. Punctuating the periods of work they have found a working year which contained literally dozens of saints' days and other religious holidays, holidays for communal celebration and holidays for other purposes. One English medieval source suggests that the regular working year amounted to only forty-four weeks. And when one adds to these seasonal interruptions the periodic work breaks attributed to moments in the life cycle (baptism, confirmations, marriages, funerals, and so on), pilgrimages, the "off season," games, political diversions, and numerous other occasions, one could well arrive at an estimation of one-third of the year being "leisure."

Not only did this free time punctuate the working year, moreover; diversions of various sorts also seem to have penetrated, or rather to have been a natural part of the work rhythm itself. We tend to be accustomed to sharper divisions: regular hours for work and defined periods of relief (with coffee breaks as a kind of no-man's-land in between). Traditional conceptions of the work rhythm might thus seem strange to us indeed, for what we find looking closely at traditional Europe is that the firm separation which we build between work and sociability simply did not exist. Instead, there often appears to be a partial integration of the two. In addition to the observance of Saint-Monday (a kind of unofficial holiday taken at the beginning of the week by some workers who usually spent the time drinking) we find all kinds of nonwork activity—singing, drinking, dancing, gossiping, and the like—guiltlessly part of the working day. On some days workers seemed to have worked extremely hard and long, as if to catch up for time lost or meet some deadline; on other days, probably too in other seasons, their work seems at first glance to be shot through with leisure.

Every historian must be both a collector and a taxonomist; having gathered his material he must also examine and classify it. Undertaking this second task with the leisure specimens just referred to, however, it becomes questionable whether our discoveries are in fact what they seem to be. Leisure, it should be remembered, is free activity, determined by individuals who make a choice independent of direct obligations of work, family, or society. Now virtually all of the nonwork activities which have been mentioned fall outside this category. Rather they seem to find their natural home in a communal or family context. This is where they arise and derive their form. Folk dancing, singing songs together with the unmarried young people of the village, celebrating the day of the shoemaker's patron saint, the baptismal feast—all of these activities are deeply rooted in custom and habit. What goes on is strictly regulated by a set of rules which approximates that of a ritual; the order in which things are done, the words which are spoken, and the reactions which people have are all closely prescribed. Therefore, instead of referring to such time spent not working as "leisure," we would prefer instead to use the term "sociability," because when the artisans or field laborers were not actually doing productive work they were talking with one another, interacting within the context of some larger and strictly defined community. These activities are a traditional part of communal life and make little sense outside it. They are, of course, a diversion from labor and they were certainly a welcome relief from toil; but they do not, for all of that, take place free from direct obligation. In our sense, then, they are not leisure activities.

It is possible to identify some kinds of activities which do fit our definition and which can be found in the fabric of traditional European social life. One of the distinguishing features of the life-style of the European aristocracy ever since the tenth or eleventh century was the indulgence in leisure practices such as the playing of a musical instrument, reading for pleasure, or perhaps even writing poetry. These practices did not occur in a communal context, and were not a part of an intricate structure of obligation. Such pastimes served in part to differentiate a tiny privileged sector from the rest of society. The life of leisure, or a life with at least some leisure, became a conspicuous goal towards which a few could aspire. But not many were able to attain it. For the overwhelming majority life was continually lived within the close framework of communal regulation and direction. Here and there, however, such as with playing cards, for example, one finds common people indulging in genuine leisure pursuits. Almost invariably these were attacked by the authorities (indeed, this is how we have come to know about them), and they certainly appear as exceptions to the rule. Leisure, it seems clear, was not for the masses.

As we know, this did not last forever. Since the eighteenth century, beginning in England, Western society has undergone changes of vast proportions, transforming every aspect of life, including conception and use of time. Historians used to speak about the significantly shorter working periods which over the long run industrialism afforded the average man; the amount of leisure time, it was sometimes argued, grew steadily with technological progress and the growing freedom from necessity. Present investigations of work rhythms in the early stages of industrialization, however, have cast doubt upon this proposition, and have suggested on the contrary that progress brought about a much more cruel discipline for the laboring masses, at least until the second half of the nineteenth century in Europe.[3] Sebastian de Grazia has even argued that the overall length of

3. See E. P. Thompson, "Time, Work-Discipline, and Industrial Capital-

the working period may have changed very little in the course of time.[4] But even if the quantitative rearrangement over this period was not significant, the qualitative changes were unquestionably so. Here we find the basis for our argument about the emergence of leisure.

Three factors were particularly important in generating leisure for the masses. First, industrial work rhythms led to an untangling of work and popular amusement. The kind of interpenetration of the two which we have observed as characteristic of traditional society was no longer possible in the routinized and regimented structure of work which was emerging. To an ever greater extent, from the beginning of the industrial period, one worked during work time, and in whatever time was left over one could take one's leisure. And although this leisure did not perhaps amount to much in terms of duration, activities which did take place then were freed, so to speak, from the regulative association with work. Rather than singing along with the other field workers, one did one's job and also joined a workers' singing club; rather than drinking with the other stonemasons during a break or on Mondays, one worked steadily all day and then drank at the neighborhood pub when and with whom one chose. In both examples the new element is choice.

Urbanization is the second generator of leisure. One of the most dramatic migrations in the long history of European man was the great movement from country to town, so intimate a part of the broad process of modernization to which we have referred. Towns and cities had always been population magnets for their surrounding territories, and even beyond, but never were the movements of population so massive or so extensive as from the beginning of the nineteenth century. Not only did urban centers grow, moreover, their cultural influences spread and diffused throughout hitherto isolated country, interrupting the life rhythms which had endured for generations. Now all of this had a decisive impact on the kind of traditional communities which had been the focal point of nonwork activity. Local com-

---

ism," *Past and Present* 38 (December 1967): 56–97; Sidney Pollard, *The Genesis of Modern Management* (Harmondsworth, Eng.: Penguin Books, 1968), Ch. 5.

4. Sebastian de Grazia, *Of Time, Work, and Leisure* (Garden City, N. Y.: Doubleday Anchor Books Edition, 1964).

munities were shattered in this process, both by the loss of members who moved away and by the loss of regulatory authority which an older tradition had once provided. Individuals caught up in this process were far less subject to the controls and obligations of custom. And among those aspects of life once ruled by custom, as we have seen, was the disposition of nonwork time. One must clearly beware of exaggerating the completeness of this process or the suddenness of its impact. Within both rural and urban communities much the same thing was happening, and the change was obviously due not so much to an urban environment per se but rather to a *modern* urban environment, itself generated by other forces more difficult to discern. But leisure can be seen growing in the environment of a newly urbanized society, thriving in the weakness of communal restraints. Where once the ritual of courtship had been organized by peasants and country dwellers since time immemorial, in the cities there now appeared few rules at all; and where the Lenten season had prescribed for rural folk a whole range of practices, feasts, and processions, the modern urban dweller seemed more and more to participate or not according to his whim or inclination.

Lastly, it is possible to speak of the commercialization of leisure. Urbanization and a new rhythm of work helped create a demand for leisure by eroding traditional constraints on the utilization of nonwork time; the supplying of leisure became at the same time the task of various agencies, from cabaret owners to bicycle manufacturers, from popular writers to sporting entrepreneurs. In literature, in the arts, and in various forms of popular recreation the eighteenth and even more the nineteenth century saw the development of a mass consuming public and hence a system of mass distribution. Dance halls, circulating libraries, museums, cinema, vacations, spectator sports, and many more facilities provided a dazzling range of choice for the practitioner of leisure. Meeting the demand, of course, the purveyors of popular culture created more demand, especially once mass advertising was enlisted in the second half of the nineteenth century. On the eve of the First World War the foundations of a powerful leisure business were laid, and the edifice would grow spectacularly ever after.

In brief outline, this is the story of the emergence of leisure. The articles which follow enlarge upon this theme, and fill in some gaps in historical analysis. They will not, however, do more than provide a sketch of a development which is still, of course, very much under way. We are really trying to describe a process which has not yet run its course, and whose effects cannot yet be seen in perspective. However, it is never too early to begin. Each of us is the product of history, we are accustomed to say. We seldom think of this when we speculate idly on the "good life," or, more simply, when we go to the movies, read a book, or listen to music. But how we have come to do these things is an interesting story. Knowing something about it tells us something about ourselves.

The Public, Literature, and the Arts in the Eighteenth Century

J. H. PLUMB

We have referred to commercialization as one of the principal generators of leisure. In the following selection, by the eminent British historian J. H. Plumb, this process is seen at work in eighteenth-century England. Here was clearly the leading edge of the development of a "leisure industry," for the changes which Plumb describes took some time to make themselves felt on the Continent. Still, it would be possible to point to similar beginnings elsewhere. Plumb notes that what is at issue is really a cultural revolution, a far-reaching societal transformation the roots of which may be found as early as the Renaissance and Reformation. If this is true, then we are not dealing with changes wrought by *industrialization,* whose principal impact was to

SOURCE: J. H. Plumb, "The Public, Literature, and the Arts in the Eighteenth Century," from *The Triumph of Culture: Eighteenth-Century Perspectives,* eds. Paul Fritz and David Williams (Toronto: A. M. Hakkert, 1972). Copyright © 1972 by J. H. Plumb. Reprinted by permission of the author and publisher.

come only in the nineteenth century. We are dealing rather with a new way of organizing society, itself made possible by important kinds of social change. The growth of leisure is thus seen as linked to a much wider series of issues, which it is the task of social history to illuminate.

Most of us are conscious of the great waves of change which are bearing along the present generation—science and technology, race relations, sexual habits, women's liberation, the revolution of the adolescents. Some are exhilarated as they ride the crest, others fearful that they will be dashed against the rocky shore. Few look back, fewer still realize that the wave they are riding has been lifting and cresting for centuries. None of our present day revolutions has a short ancestry and even that cultural revolution in which we take a certain pride has its origins long ago—its seedbed in the fifteenth century. Its early childhood was certainly long and arduous; lasting longer than one might have expected, but after some 300 years it burst into vigorous manhood in England in the eighteenth century.

By cultural revolution I mean that process by which literature and the arts have ceased to be the preoccupation of small, specialized elites and have become available for the mass of society to enjoy. For most of human history there have been two cultures—no, not science and the arts, but the culture of the governing aristocracies and the popular culture of the peasantry. This is as true of China as of Europe. From the late seventeenth century a mass culture, belonging essentially to the middle class, developed, which, if it did not quite obliterate the other two, drove them into smaller and smaller social enclaves. This transformation required three conditions—technological advance, considerable dissemination of wealth, and, by no means last, freedom. Without printing there could have been no cultural revolution. It seems to me we always undervalue an invention without which the intellectual achievements of the modern world could never have taken place.[1] Before 1450 there had been several renaissances, propitious times when knots of scholars had been actively encouraged to recover and to study the works of the ancients. But so long as the culture was scribal, such successes as they had could be lost, easily overlooked or forgotten, because they were bound to be enshrined in a small number of manuscripts. For example, John the Deacon exposed the forgery of the Donation of Constantine in the year A.D. 1000, but his work, which only existed in a few copies, was forgotten, whereas the exposure by Lorenzo Valla 400 years later was printed in what for a copied MS would have been a very large edition.[2] It became widely available, not to a handful of scholars, but to hundreds. Similarly, within a scribal culture errors tended to multiply, for copyists' mistakes were inevitable, whereas in print texts gradually, but steadily, improved in accuracy. But mainly, of course, print made books available, whereas manuscripts had rarely been so. A monastic library of 300 books was in the Middle Ages a very large library:[3] by 1600,300 books was not exceptional for a modest country gentleman of bookish tastes. Furthermore, the monastic library would have been composed almost entirely of religious books and a few encyclopedias,

1. This view is substantiated in a series of important articles by Elizabeth Eisenstein, "Some Conjectures about the Impact of Printing on Western Society and Thought: A Preliminary Report," *Journal of Modern History* 40 (1968): 1–56; "The Advent of Printing and the Problem of the Renaissance," *Past and Present* 45 (1969): 18–89; "The Advent of Printing in Current Historical Literature: Notes and Comments on an Elusive Transformation," *American Historical Review* 75 (1970): 727–743. To some extent Professor Eisenstein's case suffers a little from overemphasis. See the doubts raised by T. K. Rabb in *Past and Present* 52 (1971): 135–140. See also Eisenstein's reply, *ibid.*, pp. 140–144.

2. J. H. Plumb, *The Death of the Past* (London, 1969), pp. 79 n. 1, 82.

3. N. R. Ker, *Medieval Libraries of Great Britain. A List of Surviving Books*, 2d ed. (London, 1964), p. xi.

whereas the country gentleman's library, by 1600, would have ranged over history, geography, the classics, as well as divinity. The wide diffusion of secular knowledge could not have taken place without printing: also continuing self-education became possible to a degree that was unthinkable for a purely scribal culture. Printing, therefore, provided the spring to the wide diffusion of literature. And not only literature, but also painting, first through the woodcut and then the etching. And, of course, music too. Think of the boredom and labor involved in copying down every song that one enjoyed or every piece of instrumental music that one wished to play. This technological basis has to be stressed, for what it unleashed was in a sense so slow in developing that its revolutionary significance is often overlooked.

The exploitation of printing was curiously slow. Even two hundred years after its invention, the exploitation of its possibilities as far as a mass audience was concerned had not made much progress. Take the London of Pepys.[4] There was only one daily paper—*The London Gazette*—which contained official matters relating to the Court—proclamations, decrees, promotions, and the like, and a little very stale foreign news. Pepys had to go, and almost every day he went, to the Royal Exchange to pick up gossip from foreign merchants to learn what was happening in Europe. Similarly he would spend half an hour or so at Westminster Hall in search of news of the happenings at Court or in Parliament. He haunted taverns, not only because he loved wine, but also because he was avid for the news which was often to be found there. If you happened to live out of London, of course, the situation was worse. A rich man could subscribe to a manu-

4. For the London of Pepys, see the new edition of *The Diary of Samuel Pepys*, eds. R. C. Latham and W. Matthews, 5 vols. to date (London, 1970–). Also J. H. Plumb, "The Public and Private Pepys," *The Saturday Review* (October 24, 1970), p. 29. Reprinted in Plumb, *In the Light of History* (London, 1972).

script letter sent to him by a journalist who, like Pepys, did the rounds and then summarized what he learned for his country correspondents.[5] In consequence it was a world of surprising ignorance, alive with rumors, wonders, and marvels. For Pepys, as for most of his dilettante friends, books were precious objects rather than tools—carefully and beautifully bound they were stored in handsome locked bookcases. Still, books were available; large libraries, such as the Earl of Sunderland's, not uncommon, and reading as a pastime, as well as a scholarly pursuit, was well established.

The London of Pepys was not culturally exciting. Certainly prints of pictures were available, and Pepys bought many, but they were expensive, the editions small, and there were not many dealers. Pictures by great masters were rarely to be seen, except by the possessor and his friends. The only easily available pictures for a man or a woman who could afford to dress well were to be seen at the Royal palaces. Charles II was very accessible to his subjects and any well-dressed person could get inside the public rooms of Whitehall or Windsor. For the vast majority of men and women, however, paintings were unknown, apart from an amateur portrait by a local artist or a painted inn sign. In music they were a little better served. Even during the Commonwealth church organs had been built and Cromwell himself was fond of music. But public music, apart from church music, was exceptional. The first English opera, *The Siege of Rhodes,* was in effect a play with musical interludes. *The Tempest,* too, was turned by Shadwell into a semimusical entertainment and occasionally there were musical divertimenti in the theater. There were no concerts, few public paid perfor-

5. For a typical newsletter, see S. H. Le Fleming MSS, 1890, Historical Manuscripts Commission, 12th Report, Appendix, Part 7, London, pp. 305–307. For two official newsletter series, see Peter Fraser, *The Intelligence of the Secretaries of State and Their Monopoly of Licensed News, 1660–1688* (Cambridge, 1956), pp. 147–152.

mances until the very end of the century. Although popular, the restored theater of Charles II was poverty-stricken, new plays rare, most were badly acted and vilely produced. Addicted as Pepys was, he was but rarely pleased by what he saw.[6] And theaters were small and sparse. And in the provinces, of course, nonexistent. There, one was lucky to enjoy the antics of a few strolling players in a barn. Again, in the country one made one's own music or hired, as Sir Robert Walpole's father did, a pair of fiddlers for an evening for a shilling to play country dances.[7] The cultural poverty of late seventeenth-century England was vast—no newspapers, no public libraries, no theaters outside London, no concerts anywhere, no picture galleries of any kind, no museums, almost no botanical gardens, and no organized sports. Race meetings happened when gentlemen wagered their horses against each other; football—little better than a riot—occurred on various feast days between villages, prizefighters were matched, like racehorses, by gentlemen.[8] Nor could the mind be extended by travel, unless one was very rich. Only

6. See Latham and Matthews, *The Diary of Samuel Pepys*, 1: 309–310. December 5, 1660: "I dined at home and after dinner went to the New Theatre and there I saw *The Merry Wifes of Windsor* acted. The humors of the country gentleman and the French Doctor very well done: but the rest poorly and Sir J. Falstaffe as bad as any." Vol. 2: 175. September 9, 1661: ". . . thence to Salisbury Court playhouse, where was acted the first time *Tis pitty shee's a whore*—a simple play and ill acted." *Ibid.*, p. 202. October 26, 1661: ". . . I to the Theatre and there saw *The Country Captaine*, the first time that it hath been acted this 25 years—a play of my Lord Newcastles, but so silly a play as in all my life I never saw, and the first that ever I was weary of in my life." *Ibid.*, p. 223. November 29, 1661: ". . . I to the Theatre . . . and there saw *Love at first sight*, a play of Mr. Killigrew, and the first time that it hath been acted since before the troubles; and great expectations there was, but I find the play to be a poor thing; and so I perceive everybody else do."

7. See J. H. Plumb, "The Walpoles: Father and Son," in *Men and Places* (London, 1963), pp. 121–146.

8. Dennis Brailsford, *Sport and Society: Elizabeth to Anne* (London, 1969), pp. 205–206, 213.

the aristocratic young could afford to travel to improve their minds. Culturally the seventeenth century was circumscribed to a most remarkable degree. Much more so, one might add, than China of the same date.

Within 100 years this had almost totally changed, and we can see our own cultural world staring at us in embryo, for it was in the eighteenth century that culture began to develop a mass audience and to take the technology of printing to its furthest commercial limits. Leisure and culture became a profitable speculation in which more and more capital was sunk—an aspect of eighteenth-century economic growth almost totally ignored by economic historians. The potentiality for such a development became manifest, however, in that culturally barren world of Pepys. The Civil War had provoked a mass of ephemeral publication in which every shade of religious and political opinion had been earnestly debated. This, of course, had been largely, but not entirely, confined to London and although the flood had abated with the Restoration, neither Charles II nor James II had been able to bring unlicensed printing to a halt. Nevertheless, there was a sharp decline between 1660–1688. Private manuscript newsletter services increased as print declined, but they were expensive and so limited in circulation.[9] Satires on political events and personalities tended also to circulate in manuscript or were sung by ballad singers and often not printed until years later when the danger had passed.[10] But the pamphlet war raged with vigor. The growth of coffee houses provided more centers for the dissemination of news, scandal, rumor, and argument; and so disturbing did these seem to Charles II that he contemplated suppressing them.[11] But even as early as 1670

9. Fraser, *Secretaries of State*, p. 39.

10. Elias F. Mengel, Jr., ed., *Poems on Affairs of State, 1678–1681* (New Haven and London, 1965), 2: 511.

11. J. H. Plumb, *The Growth of Political Stability in England, 1675–1725* (London, 1967), pp. 43–44.

it was clear that there was an audience—literate, very politically orientated, even though largely London based.

The first cresting of the wave came after the Revolution of 1688, helped by war, by the rage of party politics, and the lapsing of the licensing laws. With the *Post Boy* and the *Post Man,* the first nonofficial newspapers began. In 1702 the *Daily Courant* gave London its first daily newspaper. More remarkably, all of these papers flourished. There is a remarkable growth of magazines, but they splutter and die and fail to establish themselves, but they display novel features: much that they print is not in the least concerned with politics or religion, but about the conditions of life or its curiosities and most of them encourage what today would be called "audience participation." *The Athenian Oracle* and its fellows did not last, but the market was there and growing, the right ingredients had not been found. The main road to popular success was to be in the form of the periodic essay concerned with manners, social morality, and improvement. Magazines based on this mixture burgeoned in the reign of Queen Anne—Defoe's *Review,* a herculean effort by England's first journalist (he wrote it all himself), the *Medley* and the *Tatler,* which led to the greatest triumph of all, the *Spectator,* of all things a *daily* magazine, but one which so caught the public imagination that it was in demand from New England to Sumatra.[12] Addison and Steele at last found and fully exploited the new and growing middle-class audience, an audience which longed to be modish, to be aware of fashion yet wary of its excess, to participate in the world of the great yet be free from its anxieties, to feel smug and superior to provincial rusticity and old world manners, above all to be deeply respectful of the world of commerce, and honest trading. These sentiments Addison and Steele skill-

12. See Donald F. Bond's excellent and definitive edition of *The Spectator,* 5 vols. (Oxford, 1965), 1: lxxxv–lxxxvi.

fully exploited, not with a heavy morality, but by using semi-fictionalized characters such as Sir Roger de Coverley. They provided rich entertainment as well as social education. The key to their outstanding success is contained in the name, *The Spectator:* there was an audience wide enough to participate in life through literature. As T. H. Green so aptly phrased it "that special style of literature . . . which consists in talking to the public about itself. Humanity is taken as reflected in the ordinary life of men."[13] And so, on the success of the *Spectator* one might have prognosticated both the rise of the novel and the growth of a large reading public—spectators living vicariously other people's lives.

Certainly this took place, but more slowly than might have been expected. It was not until the 1740s that Richardson and Fielding began to exploit fully the possibilities of the novel. True, there had been the early successes of Defoe's *Crusoe* and Swift's *Gulliver's Travels,* but these books were nearer to fictionalized tracts than the novel which explored the field of social realism upon which Richardson and Fielding's success was based. But once launched in the forties, the novel spread rapidly. So appealing was this new vogue that, with edges softened a little and language refined, the English novel, again led by Richardson and Fielding, swept France in the 1740s and 50s. As London was full of commercially minded printers, novels, not, however, cheap novels, poured from the presses. Most was imitative trash, meant to fill the idle hours of middle-class women and superior servant girls.[14] But the public was there, more numerous than could have been forecast in the late seventeenth century. Just how

13. Ian Watt, *The Rise of the Novel: Studies in Defoe, Richardson, and Fielding* (Berkeley and Los Angeles: University of California Press, 1967), p. 51. (Quoting from: "Estimate of the Value and Influence of Works of Fiction in Modern Times," *The Works of T. H. Green,* ed. R. L. Nettleship, 3: 27.)

14. *Ibid.,* pp. 43–47.

big this new reading public was is hard to estimate. Editions were not large—the *Spectator* was usually printed in 3,000 copies.[15] Even a very popular paper such as the *Craftsman* at the height of political excitement in the 1730s rarely, if ever, rose beyond 10,000 copies.[16] Estimates, such as Dr. Johnson's, give the most popular of all monthly periodicals, *The Gentleman's Magazine*, at no more than 10,000 copies.[17] And the bulk of the public who bought the newspapers, magazines, and books lived in London. However, it must be remembered that newspapers and magazines were provided, not only in coffee houses, but also in most taverns; and in the early decades of the eighteenth century coffee houses spread to the major provincial cities. Again, reading aloud was popular, not only to the assembled adults in a family drawing room, but also by the literate to the illiterate. There are plenty of astonished travelers' reports of workingmen grouped around one who could read to them the latest news of war and politics.[18] And it is to the twenties and thirties that we can trace the beginnings not of the very first circulating libraries—some of them date back to the seventeenth century—but to the rapid exploitation of the circulating library as a profitable line for booksellers. They too spread outwards from London, first to the fashionable spas—Tunbridge Wells and Bath—and then on to major provincial cities—Bristol, Norwich, and indeed beyond.[19] By 1760 every town of any

15. Bond, *The Spectator*, 1: xxv–xxvii.

16. J. H. Plumb, *Sir Robert Walpole*, 2 vols. (London, 1956 and 1961), vol. 2, *The King's Minister*, pp. 141–143, 179–182.

17. For Dr. Johnson's estimate of *The Gentleman's Magazine*, see Watt, *Rise of the Novel*, p. 51. For the circulation of newspapers and periodicals in general see James R. Sutherland, "The Circulation of Newspapers and Literary Periodicals, 1700–30," *The Library*, 4th ser., 15 (1935): 110–124.

18. César de Saussure, *A Foreign View of England in the Reigns of George I and George II*, trans. Van Muyden (London, 1902), p. 162. Also Plumb, *Walpole*, vol. 1, *The Making of a Statesman*, p. 31.

19. Paul Kaufman, "The Community Library: A Chapter in English Social

size in the West Midlands had at least one circulating library
and they could be found flourishing in moderately large villages. Mr. Hanbury of Church Langton, a small village in
Leicestershire, was advertising his circulating library in the
Coventry newspapers in 1760 (although his village was some
fifteen to twenty miles away).[20] And there was a more exclusive and private development—the Book Club—in which
twenty or thirty like-minded men banded together to exchange books and sometimes to meet for a social evening in
order to discuss them. This was largely a provincial development, but one which as yet has been scarcely explored.[21]
Tainworth (a small town in the Midlands, not far from Dr.
Johnson's Lichfield), had several well-established book clubs
by the 1770s, most of them associated with local taverns. It
is true, however, that these media cater largely for the middle class, professional men and women, or the minor gentry
who had to spend so much of their lives isolated in the countryside. However, it would be wrong to think that the growth
of publishing and the increase in the reading public, symbol-
ized by the rise of the novel, was confined only to the leisured
middle class. Eighteenth-century men and women of the
lower middle class were eager to participate in the growing
affluence of England through self-improvement. They lusted
for education: for themselves, for their children. 1744 saw

History," *Transactions of the American Philosophical Society* 57, part 7
(1967): 50–53. George Barton of Huntingdon was advertising his circulating
library in the St. Ives, St. Neots, and Peterborough newspapers in 1718.
Ibid., pp. 8–9. Also J. H. Plumb, "Reason and Unreason in the Eighteenth
Century: The English Experience," *William Andrews Clark Memorial Library* (University of California, Los Angeles, 1971), p. 15.

20. John Money, "Taverns, Coffee Houses, and Clubs: Local Politics and
Popular Articulacy in the Birmingham Area in the Age of the American
Revolution," *Historical Journal* 14, no. 1 (1971): 15–47.

21. For book clubs, see Kaufman, "The Community Library," pp. 26–28.
Also Paul Kaufman, "English Book Clubs and Their Role in Social History,"
Libri 14: 1–31.

the real foundation of something today everywhere taken for granted—the production of books for children's education and enjoyment. John Newbery published his *A Little Pretty Pocket Book* to teach the alphabet: it was beautifully printed and illustrated, priced sixpence, and as an extra selling gimmick—for an extra twopence you could have a ball for your son and a pincushion for your daughter.[22] Of course, there had been children's books before this—hornbooks for the alphabet teaching and chapbooks that related fairy stories which, however, I expect were read as much by country folk as by their children, but there had been no systematic and carefully designed children's reading books. Newbery continued to print such books with exceptional success—*and profit.* His *Art of Arithmetic* and *Art of Writing* enjoyed a vast public and he was the first publisher to devise a magazine for young children, *The Lilliputian Magazine,* published in 1751—a venture which, alas, failed. Newbery—a typical eighteenth-century entrepreneur—had his eye on the middle-class market. Even at sixpence his wares were well beyond the means of everyone lower than a tradesman.[23] Nevertheless, other publishers were attempting to push printed matter to the very limits of literacy—not only in cheap chapbooks and penny ballads or Old Moore's prognostications at a halfpenny a time, but by the "partbook"— a device which has had a renewed vogue in Britain this last five or six years. The partbook has two great advantages. The price of a bit of a book can be kept within the means of the poorest section of the market. On the other hand, the profit

22. John Newbery, *A Little Pretty Pocket Book,* ed. M. F. Thwaite (Oxford, 1966), p. 2.

23. For John Newbery, see Charles Welsh, *A Bookseller of the Last Century. Being some Account of the life of John Newbery and the Books he published, with a notice of the later Newberys* (London, 1875), pp. 106–116. M. F. Thwaite, *From Primer to Pleasure* (London, 1963), pp. 40–51. F. J. H. Darton, *Children's Books in England,* 2d ed. (London, 1958), pp. 122–140.

is enormous, for the total cost of the book soars well beyond what it would be if sold in a single volume.[24] In a desultory way, it had been tried for ballads and poems in Queen Anne's day (a dreadful poem entitled "A Journey to Hell" had struggled through three parts in 1705), but the boom time came in the twenties and thirties when histories, encyclopedias, gazeteers, and even the Bible were produced in penny and twopenny parts. The avidity for knowledge to which this was the commercial response caught the eye of the provincial newspapers which were being established at this time and more often at their wit's end for material.

These newspapers had begun in the boom time of Queen Anne's wars, but hit the doldrums after the Peace of Utrecht, when many went to the wall. The need for newspapers remained in the provinces largely for a vehicle for advertisement—itself an indication of rising demand—also the eagerness for national and foreign news did not entirely disappear. A few successful newspapers kept going on a diet of news, sex, and wonders of all kinds, such as women giving birth to rabbits and the like. Indeed they exploited the untutored appetites of their naive audience with the skill of the tabloid press today, similarly dressing up their pornography in pious condemnation. But they kept alive, and not only kept alive, but steadily proliferated. By 1760 there were thirty-five provincial newspapers, most of them well established.[25] They give us insight into the increasingly vigorous cultural life of eighteenth-century England with their advertisements for schools, for dancing masters, with their news of itinerant salesmen bringing the London fashions, with their notices of assemblies and balls and of their accounts of weekly debates

24. R. M. Wiles, *Serial Publication in England before 1750* (Cambridge, 1957), pp. 133–194.

25. G. A. Cranfield, *The Development of the Provincial Newspaper, 1700–1760* (Oxford, 1962), pp. 1–28. R. M. Wiles, *Freshest Advices: Early Provincial Newspapers in England* (Columbus, Ohio, 1965), p. 373.

at the local Conversation Clubs. It is from these papers that we learn of the popularity of lectures on science, of the frequency of debate of political and social questions. And we learn, too, of the hunger for the theater, for music, and for the metropolitan sophistications of life. We glimpse, through them, the birth of that culture-hungry, consumer society which has grown so fast in the last 200 years.

Only the Netherlands had undergone so thorough a commercial revolution as England did between 1688–1760, but England's population was larger and its revolution more extensive. Long wars stimulated production and by the middle of the century world overseas commerce was beginning to pay handsome dividends. Not only was an exceptionally buoyant home market created, but the burden of labor became much lighter for the men and women who belonged to the minor gentry, the affluent middle class, or even to a lesser extent the shopkeepers and tradesmen who lived on the fringe of the middle classes. For the first time there was a leisured middle class to exploit—not rich enough to enjoy their pleasures as the aristocracy had traditionally enjoyed theirs, but longing for the same cultural activities. The first exploitation of this new market came through printers, publishers, and writers—of that there can be little doubt. And the stimulus created by this and the new techniques of exploitation which publishers and the bookselling trade devised—newspapers, magazines, libraries, book clubs, and the like helped, too, the general exploitation of leisure. Books and papers devoted to manners ran endless essays on the theater, on music, on dancing, its temptations as well as its delights. Even by satirizing the fashionable world they whetted an appetite for it. But the fascination for the social historian is the rapidity with which both the hunger for culture and the increase in leisure were exploited in the eighteenth century—and, of course, exploited at a profit: for the first time the combination of leisure and culture becomes an important industry.

Perhaps one of the most remarkable changes took place in painting and the decorative arts. Unfortunately one can only touch briefly on this huge subject. By the eighteenth century engraving already had a long history, but it had largely been confined to small editions of pictures by great artists which quickly disappeared into the cabinets of the cognoscenti. The only other common engravings were portraits of the great— usually the King, his family, and his courtiers. There were also a few allegorical engravings, as well as cheap woodcuts and numerous political satires, but so far the art of engraving had not found its *Spectator*. It did so in William Hogarth,[26] whose *Harlot's Progress* had a similar impact and for similar reasons—a mixture of social realism, dramatically presented, with high-toned morality. Twelve hundred subscribers were delighted with their copies of *Harlot's Progress*; edition after edition flowed from the plates and within twelve months there were eight pirated versions. Hogarth was so enraged that he promoted a Copyright Act which successfully passed the House of Commons in 1735 and gave designers and engravers fifteen years exclusive use of their own productions. A new series by Hogarth, *The Rake's Progress*, soon followed, with a like prodigious success. As Fielding wrote in 1740, "A sober family should be no more without them than without *The Whole Duty of Man* in the house." Indeed, they became the favorite decoration of middle-class staircases and dining rooms. Naturally Hogarth followed up his success with a stream of good prints, and imitators abounded. Engraving became immensely profitable. Pictures by English artists from Richardson to Gainsborough were quickly engraved and as quickly sold and so a middle class who could never afford an original modern or old master could festoon their drawing rooms with what was modish in the world of art. By

26. For Hogarth, see Ronald Paulson, *Hogarth: His Life, Art, and Times*, 2 vols. (New Haven, 1971). Also J. H. Plumb, "Hogarth's Progress," *The New York Review of Books* 17, no. 10 (December 16, 1971): 27–28.

the 1780s, England was exporting prints throughout Western Europe—consignments to Spain, even, reaching as much as 15,000 pounds at a time. And in London and provincial cities, the print shop became as familiar as a grocer or a draper— and probably more profitable.

Hogarth's act not only stimulated the engraving of fine pictures, but also of satire and caricature—often vicious, often obscene, usually pertinent and sometimes funny— these political cartoons became a symbol of the freedom of English life. In the 1760s when Lord Bute, the favorite of George III, became the object of intense hatred, there were over 400 derisory prints made about him and one, *The Repeal or the Funeral of Miss Annie Stamp,* dealing with the Stamp Act, sold approximately 16,000 copies.[27] The vitality of this aspect of popular art has rarely been equaled and in Bunbury, Gillray, and Rowlandson England produced pictorial satirists of outstanding genius. In no other country could a satirist of the great live both in affluence and public esteem. Elsewhere, except perhaps in Frederick the Great's Prussia or the truly independent America, he would have been clapped in jail. But participation in art went beyond the cheap engraving—the obvious success and acclaim of British artists made many a young man's pencil twitch and the leisured young ladies of London fancied themselves at drawing and watercolors, dexterity at which became almost as much a mark of gentility as skill in dancing the minuet.

The rich, of course, grew as ever thirsty for costly canvases to adorn their walls. There had been collectors since the days of James I and beyond, but they were few and aristocratic. Now picture collectors became a commonplace in London and the market was as flooded as New York in the twenties with old masters, good, bad, and indifferent. Sir Robert Wal-

27. *Ex. inf.* John Brewer.

pole, like any Mellon, set the pace and drove up prices to record heights,[28] but acquired over 300 splendid pictures which, bought by Catherine the Great from his grandson, became the foundation of the Hermitage collection in Leningrad. But it was this century that began that vast accumulation of paintings which could not be matched by any nation until America entered the art market in the twentieth century. Such a vigorous appetite for painting naturally stimulated other arts—sculpture, architecture, and the decorative arts, and here again, England achieved a mass middle-class audience that other European nations singularly failed to acquire. But one example must suffice.

The European aristocracy had become increasingly entranced by Chinese porcelain at the turn of the eighteenth century and alchemists and chemists had sought for the materials to make it in Europe, a search that ended with Böttger at Meissen. Other factories and other types of porcelain—soft and hard—quickly followed this initial discovery. The porcelain so made was exceedingly expensive and was designed almost entirely with the noble or luxury market in view. Indeed it proved almost impossible for porcelain factories to survive without lavish royal patronage—attempts in England—Chelsea, Bow, Longton Hall, all went bankrupt, and Louis XV had to rescue the French factories at Vincennes and Sèvres, at times acting as his own salesman.[29] It took the genius of Josiah Wedgwood to exploit properly the huge market that lay beyond the fringes of the aristocratic world. He devised or took over new materials and inventions —basalt, agate, jasper—produced good and expensive vases

28. For Sir Robert Walpole's collecting activities, see Plumb, *Walpole*, 2: 86–87.

29. For this mania for porcelain, see J. H. Plumb, "The Royal Porcelain Craze," *Horizon* (Summer 1968), pp. 80–89. Reprinted in Plumb, *In the Light of History*.

that could adorn the mantlepieces of the great, pushed his way into royal patronage, and at the same time produced vases and flowerpots at prices which the middle class could afford—not cheap because that would not have flattered their egos, but *expensive within their means*. And so before the end of the eighteenth century a symbol of middle-class culture was as much a Wedgwood vase as a copy of the *Spectator* or Hogarth's *Marriage à la Mode*.[30] And this was true of so many of the decorative arts in England—furniture such as the French *èbenistes* made for the European aristocracy were beyond the means of lawyers in Norwich or doctors in Bristol or coal traders in Newcastle but, with the elegance retained, indeed improved, but the decoration severely modified, the chairs and commodes and tables of Sheraton and Hepplewhite brought a delight to middle-class living which flattered by its reflection of aristocratic taste.[31]

Increasingly in the eighteenth century the aristocracy, the gentry, and the financiers became very rich indeed, whilst the middle-class living standards steadily became less precarious and more affluent. Some of this wealth in the towns, large and small, seeped down to the shopkeepers, tradesmen, innkeepers, and the like. It would be quite wrong to forget the welter of poverty and destitution that still embraced in a deathly vise-like grip the majority of the population, which remained illiterate as well as barbarous, and for whom food, shelter, and clothing consumed all of their pitiful

30. For Josiah Wedgwood, see the important series of articles by Neil McKendrick, especially "Josiah Wedgwood: An Eighteenth-Century Entrepreneur in Salesmanship and Marketing Techniques," *Economic History Review* 12 (1959–1960): 408–433; "Josiah Wedgwood and Thomas Pentley: An Inventor-Entrepreneur partnership in the Industrial Revolution," *Transactions of the Royal Historical Society* (1964): 1–33; "The Enigmatic Urn," *Horizon* (November 1963), pp. 63–65.

31. The eighteenth century saw the first real growth of leisure shopping; hence the development of the bow window for shops which enabled more goods to be set out to catch the expectant eye.

earnings, yet the prosperous middle class was sufficiently
numerous to begin to change the taste and culture of English
society.

So far I have discussed this cultural explosion in terms of
media—the spread of printing, of the etching, or of the exploitation of the market for more sophisticated goods. But
there is always the world of active pleasure, which is just as
important as the more passive pursuits. For the first time in
the eighteenth century there were sufficient people of sufficient leisure for their exploitation to become professional-
ized. The prelapsarian myth cultivated by Leavis and his
school, and also encouraged by many historians, has pictured
the eighteenth and nineteenth century worlds, in contrast to
our own, as a world in which cultural participation was the
rule: in which people made their own music, made their own
games, and were not in their idle moments the passive recipi-
ents.

In all societies there is a vast amount of self-made culture
—one has only to think of the large number of amateur rock
groups or choirs or orchestras or chamber music ensembles,
to say nothing of amateur theatricals in our own day, and the
same is true of sport. Nevertheless there is a marked change
between the seventeenth and eighteenth centuries and once
again England led the way, even if it did not always initiate
the changes. An excellent example lies in music. Almost everyone who takes delight in music wants to make it. Elizabethan England was full of songsters, full of lute players.
Nevertheless, as I mentioned earlier, apart from sacred music, there was practically none that could be publicly heard.
The best one could hope for was an interlude at the theater,
or to find a tavern where a girl or boy could sing a country
tune or play the fiddle for a country dance. Little or no music
was published. The change after 1688 is dramatic. It is true
that for the next fifty years orchestras and great musicians,
composers as well as executants, were largely supported by

aristocratic patronage—one has only to think of the Duke of Chandos's great orchestra at Cannons, for whom first Handel and then Pepusch composed—but public rooms or clubs, open to subscribers, began to develop with rapidity in the reign of Anne and the first Georges—some, like Thomas Britton's—catering for a quite humble public. He converted the loft of his coal house where, for a subscription of ten shillings a year and a penny for coffee, one could listen not only to the great English composers, Byrd, Gibbons, Purcell, Locke, and Blow, but also to concerti by Corelli and Vivaldi, the court music of Lully and the great German instrumentalist school of Biber and Rosenmuller.[32] Hickford's rooms in St. James's Piccadilly were more fashionable and lasted longer, closing only in 1779,[33] by which time there were a number of flourishing concert halls in London—the Hanover Square Rooms, where Mozart was first popularized, Carlisle House in Soho, the Pantheon in Oxford Street, which was also used as a theater, and Willis's Rooms, which remained in existence for well over a century. For the size of its potential audience, London was probably as well served with concert halls by 1770 as it is today.

And this was only the tip of the musical iceberg. According to Paul Henry Lang, "Toward the middle of the century almost every Town, Castle, University, and Church has its orchestra and many musical associations gathered for weekly musical exercises."[34] And the change can be seen in the fare offered by taverns: although many still provided nothing but country songs and dances, an increasing number put on orchestral concerts—Handel's Oratorio *Esther* was performed, for instance, at the Crown and Anchor Tavern—or invested

32. For Thomas Britton, see *The Oxford Companion to Music,* ed. Percy Scholes, 9th ed. (London, 1955), p. 227.

33. For Thomas Hickford, *ibid.*

34. Paul Henry Lang, *Music in Western Civilization* (London, 1942), p. 724.

in a Church organ, much to the horror of visiting foreigners, who thought it sacrilegious. As with London, so with the provinces. Starting with the famous Three Choirs' Festival (Gloucester, Worcester, Hereford) in 1713,[35] no city of any size was without its musical festivals by the second half of the century.[36] With so wide an audience, middle-class taste dominated. For proof one need only turn to the failure of aristocratically supported Italian opera in the 1720s with the incredible popular success of *The Beggar's Opera* which took London so much by storm that in the next decade over a hundred ballad operas were written and produced.[37] Again, the first burst of music publishing came after the Revolution of 1688, when Thomas Cross, John Hare, and John Walsh applied the same high pressure methods to music as was common with political pamphlets—that is, large cheap editions, as much advertising and puffing as they could find.[38] Walsh, for example, published 600 works in his first twenty-five years.[39] This was but the beginning of a deluge of printed music and there seem to have been about as many musical publishers as ordinary publishers. After 1740, London, the provinces, and Ireland doubled their numbers—London reaching the astonishing figure of over 400. Even Scotland became musical. There were six active publishers before 1740, but fifty-nine new ones established themselves before 1800.[40]

35. For this festival, see Watkins Shaw, *The Three Choirs' Festival* (Worcester, Mass., 1954).

36. Percy M. Young, *The Concert Tradition* (London, 1965). Birmingham Festival was founded in 1768; Norwich in 1770; Manchester in 1777; Handel Commemorations in London, 1784; and the Yorkshire festival in 1791.

37. John Gay, *The Beggar's Opera*, ed. Edgar V. Roberts, music ed. Edward Smith (Lincoln, Nebr., 1969).

38. Charles Humphries and William C. Smith, *Music Publishing in the British Isles* (London, 1954), p. 17.

39. *Ibid.*, p. 18.

40. *Ibid.*, pp. 49–346.

As with music, song, and dance, so with the theater. Not only did they increase in London, but the major towns and many minor ones had built theaters by 1750 and expected to see popular London plays acted by some of the leading London professionals.[41] Except for the remoter parts of England, gone forever were the days when a band of strolling comedians took over a farmer's barn for bawdy traditional farces, grotesque melodrama, and conjuring tricks, although somewhat more sophisticated mixtures of this kind were to be found in the huge manufacturing towns—Birmingham, Manchester, Leeds—in transition, as it were, to the great music halls of the nineteenth century. Music, dancing, theater—these were the cultural pastimes for which the prosperous gentry and the new leisured middle class hungered. But their houses were not large enough for private theaters, for private orchestras, or private concerts, nor had they the money to lavish on such conspicuous aristocratic functions. And so it is not surprising that market towns began to build subscription Assembly Rooms, where the social elite of the county could meet for balls, for music, for improving lectures, and of course for dramatic performances. Some assembly rooms, such as those at York, were magnificent in conception and design; others were one or two great rooms attached to the leading inn and could double up on occasion for Masonic meetings. Often the subscription was high, which at least kept out the minor shopkeepers and traders, but these Assembly Rooms mark the transitional stage between private and fully public entertainment. As culture seeped through to

41. Allardyce Nicoll, *A History of early Eighteenth-Century Drama, 1700–1750*, 2d ed. (Cambridge, Eng., 1929). For the development of the London stage see particularly pp. 271–273; for the provincial theater see p. 4. See also *idem., A History of late Eighteenth-Century Drama, 1750–1800* (Cambridge, Eng., 1927), pp. 3, 232–348. Sybil Rosenfeld, *Strolling Players and Drama in the Provinces, 1660–1765* (Cambridge, Eng., 1939).

the masses, and so became more commercially viable, these subscription rooms fell into desuetude. Many, however, remain to remind us of the elegance and sophistication of upper-class provincial life in eighteenth-century England.[42] They were, of course, the provincial equivalent of those two wonders of London—Vauxhall and Ranelagh Gardens, where one could dine, listen to music, look at excellent pictures, and of course dance, sometimes masked, sometimes not, and above all partake of that favorite eighteenth-century sport of sauntering to ogle the girls.[43]

A similar transitional stage can be seen in the growth of the town dedicated entirely to leisure or retirement—a phenomenon which is now so commonplace in the western world that it is difficult to remind oneself how recent and how significant this development is. Like the readers of the *Spectator* or *Pamela*, eighteenth-century men and women, eager for a holiday, liked to have a sound moral excuse for their enjoyment. And so the first holiday centers grew up at spas—Bath and Tunbridge Wells, quickly followed by Scarborough, Bristol Hot Springs, Cheltenham, Harrogate, Matlock, and the rest. Brighton, where one took the sea water internally, as well as externally, got off to a slow start, but roared ahead under the patronage of the Prince Regent to-

42. Typical small town assembly rooms, both beautiful eighteenth-century buildings, are those at Bury St. Edmunds and Leicester. For Leicester see Jack Simmons, "A Leicester Architect, 1752–1814," *Parish and Empire: Studies and Sketches* (London, 1952), which deals with John Johnson. The Lion Hotel, Cambridge, possessed a brilliant eighteenth-century assembly room, now demolished, that doubled as a Masonic Lodge. The early assembly room at Brighton is attached to the Old Ship Hotel.

43. For the Vauxhall Gardens see Mollie Sands, "Music Not Too Refined," *Musical Times* 91 (1950): 11–15. See also Percy M. Young, *The Concert Tradition*, p. 138. For the Ranelagh Gardens see *ibid.*, p. 140. See also E. D. Mackerness, *A Social History of English Music* (London, 1964), pp. 104–105. It was, of course, Hogarth's idea that Vauxhall Gardens should display contemporary paintings: he never missed a chance of exploiting the market; see Paulson, *Hogarth*, 1: 347–348.

ward the end of the century, when the spas themselves began slowly to decline, as men and women began to accept frankly the idea of a holiday for holiday's sake.[44] Also men and women may have become healthier as personal and social hygiene improved, for there can be no doubt that the majority of those who went to the spas in the middle of the century usually had some ailment, major or minor, which they hoped the hideous waters might cure. But the main business of spas was amusement—dancing, theater, music, and reading and, of course, flirting and making love. Just as it was a little lower down the social scale at Islington or Sadlers Wells, so were the spas nearest to London to which the tradesmen flocked.[45]

All the activities that I have so far described point to the growth of a middle-class audience—not a mass audience by our standards—but so large and growing a one that its commercial exploitation was becoming an important industry, and it was a market that had enormous potential for growth. And the seeds of future development were also occurring in one aspect of human living that historians constantly ignore —sport.

Until the eighteenth century, sport had been either for gentlemen or peasants and always something that you made for yourself. If you had a fine horse, you wagered it against your neighbor's, or if you were a racing man you congregated with other racing men at Newmarket or Doncaster and spent a week in challenging those you fancied that you could beat. But it was haphazard; there were conventions rather than rules, and few spectators except those involved in the racing

44. For Brighton, see Osbert Sitwell and Margaret Barton, *Brighton* (London, 1935). Also J. H. Plumb, "The Brighton Pavilion," *Men and Places*, pp. 80–97.

45. G. D. H. Cole, "Town Life in the Provinces," *Johnson's England: An Account of the Life and Manners of His Age*, ed. A. S. Turberville (Oxford, 1933), pp. 215–216.

or the business of racing, except maybe for a few neighboring gentlemen. But steadily throughout the century racing became properly organized—important meetings established elaborate rules drawn up for jockeys and the whole sport became regulated and disciplined—and popular. More and more spectators arrived at the courses for the purpose of watching and gambling. The Derby on Epsom Downs became a seminational event that drew tens of thousands. What was true of horse racing became true of cricket: spectators became as important as participants and special grounds— Lords, for example—were built to accommodate the crowds who wanted to watch.[46] Indeed, organized sport, which was to become a major industry in the nineteenth and twentieth centuries throughout the world, began in eighteenth-century England, a part of that selfsame exploitation of leisure which had stimulated all the arts that adorn the life of man.

Not that many contemporaries thought so: as in our days the spread of culture amongst the masses was regarded as a decline in standards. There was very sharp criticism, an uneasy feeling expressed by Hume, Johnson, Burke, Goldsmith, Reynolds, and others that the great age of artistic achievement was past and could not be recovered, that more meant worse. Like Kingsley Amis, they believed that the very act of writing for a mass audience led to coarseness and triviality

46. For horse racing, see Robert Black, *Horse Racing in England: A Synoptical View* (London, 1893); *idem., The Jockey Club and Its Founders* (London, 1891); T. A. Cook, *A History of the English Turf,* 3 vols. (London, 1905). For the grandstand at Richmond see J. Fairfax-Blakeborough, *Northern Turf History,* 3 vols. (London, 1949). What was true of horse racing was also true of boxing. The first set of rules were introduced in August 1743 by Jack Broughton, the same year he opened his amphitheater. *Boxiana,* by one of the Fancy, 3 vols. (London, 1812) 1: 49–51; 2: 9–10. Broughton usually took one-third of the takings; *Athletic Exercise or the Science of Boxing Displayed* (London, 1788), p. 17; prices were often high and in 1786 it cost one guinea to watch the championship of England. *Fistiana: or the Oracle of the Ring,* by the editor of Bell's Life in London (London, 1841), p. 33.

and to a loss of subtlety and refinement. And then, as now, the quantities of ephemeral trash could be pointed to as a sign of the age's decadence.

What was happening, of course, was the decline of two cultures and the birth of a third. In spite of the Elizabethan theater, which could and did leap across class boundaries, the culture of England had been either aristocratic or bucolic until the age of Addison and Pope. Although the whole of culture had been under the control of aristocratic patronage, the only vital part to escape that control was popular religion and its two great books, Foxe's *Martyrs* and Bunyan's *Pilgrim's Progress*. Literature, painting, and the arts, however, belonged in essentials to the aristocracy. And the peasants, of course, had their crudities—their barn dances, their traditional songs, their farces, distinct from aristocratic sophistication. The new middle-class culture grew up between both, absorbing most of what the aristocratic culture had acquired and taking a not inconsiderable amount from the peasantry. But the difference was great—and it lay in the fact of an audience that was large enough to be commercially exploited. Culture became an industry, as it still is. And there was a further dimension, alien both to aristocratic or bucolic cultures. And that was a moral earnestness, a belief that a taste for the arts led to improvement and refinement. This infuses almost every cultural activity of the eighteenth century and, indeed, was even to be a justification of organized sport—that it led to health, to manliness, to the capacity to submerge the self in the team.

And unlike the culture of the nobleman or peasant, this culture was national and poised for growth—it could absorb the lower middle class as well as the upper; in time it would reach down even to the skilled working class. Books, music, painting were no longer private, and leisure itself had become for the first time in our history an industry, and one which became for the next two centuries and probably beyond a major growth point for the world's economies.

We often think of the middle years of eighteenth-century life creating the dark satanic mills and the desperate conditions of slum life, but those selfsame decades also brought the possibility of cultural enjoyment to the mass of mankind.

Towards a History of *La Vie Intime:* The Evidence of Cultural Criticism in Nineteenth-Century Bavaria

EDWARD SHORTER

In the previous selection J. H. Plumb mentioned "freedom" as one of the principal conditions of the cultural transformation which, as we have argued, gave rise to the modern phenomenon of leisure. In the following article by Edward Shorter, a historian at the University of Toronto, we look more closely at the kind of freedom which can be seen growing deep in the soil of popular life. Shorter's evidence comes from Bavaria in the first half of the nineteenth century, from circumstances of rapid modernization which were roughly similar to those in other parts of Central, Northern, and Western Europe, and the British Isles. His focus, moreover, is on the lower classes, for whom the availability of a wider and freer range of diversions came somewhat later than

SOURCE: Edward Shorter, "Towards a History of *La Vie Intime:* The Evidence of Cultural Criticism in Nineteenth-Century Bavaria," originally published in Germany in the *Kölner Zeitschrift für Soziologie und Sozialpsychologie* 16 (1973): 530–549. Reprinted by permission of the author.

for the middle-class elements discussed by Plumb. In the case of Shorter's Bavarians commercialization obviously mattered less, and the emancipation from the cake of communal custom mattered more than for Plumb's eighteenth-century Englishmen. But for both groups the result is the same: the growing possibility of choosing new kinds of activities for nonworking time.

If we are to believe contemporaries, popular morality simply disintegrated in Bavaria during the first half of the nineteenth century. In those years complaints about the decline of virtue and the rejection of social authority were trumpeted forth with a ferocity without precedent in either the century before or in the years to follow—until the Weimar Republic.[1] This tirade against moral decay is, of course, interesting in its own right, for what it tells us about those doing the complaining, the established social elites, and especially the lower-echelon government administrators whose lamentations have been preserved in the state archives.

Yet even more compelling is the small but precious insight these windy, overwrought, self-righteous, and self-important documents may grant into changes in the lives of men and women who otherwise would have filed unnoticed through the historical record. Perhaps the great glacier of cultural rules and habits of the popular classes, normally so slow to shift, did in fact lurch a few inches forward in the period whose center of gravity is the Vormärz. In studying the modernization of *la vie intime* we should at least admit as evidence the perceptions of those educated, upper-class Bavarian administrators, who in watching dossiers on problems of public order and private morality parade across their desks became ever more outraged by what they saw.

1. On an eruption of moral outrage in 1848–1849 see Edward Shorter, "Middle-Class Anxiety in the German Revolution of 1848," *Journal of Social History* 2 (1969): 189–215.

First, we must get the definitions straight. By *la vie intime* I mean simply the principal areas of social life where an individual's self-image is likely to affect his interaction with other people: sexuality and authority. Many sexual matters (though not all) are subject to cultural operating rules, and how a person sees himself will modify inevitably his libidinal stances towards others. Self-image regulates as well the individual's sense of allegiance to social authorities, be they within the family, the workshop, the community, or the nation-state, for the greater one's awareness of the boundary line between one's own ego and the objective world, the greater the sense of personal autonomy. So *la vie intime* is that part of the ego at which the roads of sex and power intersect. The aggregate of all the specific operating rules individuals conform to in authority and sexual relationships is "popular culture." And "popular" means virtually all strata of the population beneath the level of large landowner, wholesale merchant, or educated upper middle classes in general. Within the popular classes, however, it is specifically the "lower orders," or those in dependency relationships, who will catch our eye in this essay.

What follows constitutes illustration, not verification. It goes without saying that in order to prove an important change was really underway in something like styles of clothing or dancing, systematic quantitative information would be necessary. Such dimensions of *la vie intime* are, by their very nature, enormously difficult to measure historically with data representative of the "average" experience.[2] Government records seem to offer a plausible pulley upon the curtain of silence. There were a number of interfaces between intimate

2. For a variety of more quantitative approaches to the fabric of popular life see Werner K. Blessing, "Zur Analyse politischer Mentalität und Ideologie der Unterschichten im 19. Jahrhundert: Aspekte, Methoden, und Quellen am bayerischen Beispiel," *Zeitschrift für bayerische Landesgeschichte* 34 (1971): 768–816.

behavior and bureaucratic record keeping. Like all Central European states, Bavaria had in the first half of the nineteenth century a complex of laws which made dependent on official approval whether a man could practice a trade or subdivide property, get married or live in sin with a woman, receive poor relief, or indeed move to another community. And as I pored over the dossiers on individual cases and official reports on larger policy problems of migration, employment, and local government, I acquired the impression that powerful forces were transforming the fabric of popular culture.[3] As I had hoped, this inquisitorial machinery had preserved a running commentary on popular patterns of entertainment, family life, sexual practices, and the like. Administrators would sometimes throw off these comments as *obiter dicta*, sometimes because "morality" questions had immediate policy implications. In the absence of other kinds of information the historian is forced to observe *la vie intime* through the eyes of these royal bureaucrats, men who perceived change and innovation as dissolution and decay. The trick is to penetrate this filter of outrage to the reality of social life.

Perceptions of Moral Crisis

Let these men speak for themselves. Provincial officials in Oberfranken lamented in 1833 that, "The condition of morality cannot be in general described as satisfactory." Indeed in the last three years, they claimed, things had gotten worse. There was too little parental supervision, too much illegitimacy. And public opinion had come to be less harsh against moral and criminal offenders. "Morality has, how-

3. I gratefully acknowledge the generosity of Professor Karl Bosl in this enterprise, who made both the resources of the Institute für Bayerische Geschichte available to me and shared with me his own enormous learning on the evolution of social mores.

ever, sunken most in regard to the satisfaction of the sex drive, especially in the countryside. Among all the lower classes the disregard of morality has degenerated into a limitless freedom."[4] Hard words.

But in fact morality had become an important concern of day-to-day administration. Whenever the provincial governors would travel about their realms on inspection tours, they would peer anxiously at the state of local morals and report their findings back to Munich. Franz Wilhelm, Freiherr von Asbeck, was journeying through Unterfranken in 1823 when it came to his attention that, ". . . in the village of Gossmannsdorf, Hofheim County, a great corruption of morals is raging among the inhabitants, both young and old. This writer has thus seen himself occasioned to bring the attention of the royal government to this. . . ."[5] Yet, praise be, when Ludwig, Fürst zu Oettingen-Wallerstein was visiting Füssen County in 1829 he was able to remark that morality was "very high, continually in progress. . . . The morals bear the stamp of a mountain-people. Respect for authority, a sense for order in family as in public life, self-esteem, candor with modesty and intelligence have been perceived everywhere."[6] And here is Arnold, Ritter von Link, provincial governor of Schwaben, on his 1837 tour through that province:

—Göggingen County: "morality and public safety—not commendable. Causes: the excessive settlement of too many propertyless families permitted earlier by [the patrimonial

4. All manuscript materials, unless otherwise noted, are to be found in the Bayerisches Hauptstaatsarchiv; MI designates Ministerium des Innern, MH Ministerium des Handels. MI 15396, Öffentliche Sitten. Zustand der Sittlichkeit. Auszüge aus den dreijährigen Verwaltungs Berichte, 1830–1833. I have used in all cases the names which the *Regierungsbezirke* of the Kingdom received in the reorganization of 1837.

5. MI 39092, n. 586, July 14, 1823.

6. MI 39095, May 4, 1829.

courts of] Schlipsheim and Deuringen; the vicinity of the city [Augsburg] and the numerous garrisons; the many factory workers whom the nearby hamlets supply to the city."

—Friedberg County: "condition of morals without distressing aspects. Dances limited."

—Burgau County: "morality not very commendable, especially in Burgau. . . . Dancing curtailed. [But] illegitimate births frequent."[7]

Anxiety over moral issues penetrated even to the Interior Ministry in Munich, which in 1851 issued the following decree instructing provincial officials to get the population back onto the right track:

> The necessity [for such an ordinance] has become overwhelmingly clear during the past year because of the danger which, occasioned by this evil, threatens the entire social order. [What events the government had in mind is not clear, but they had become manifest in] . . . increasing impiety, widespread laziness and pleasure-seeking, the growing disregard for law, good-breeding and morality, the widening lack of domesticity, the ever-growing overestimation of self, the newly rising indifference to the interests of the community when a question of personal advantage is involved—all these are phenomena which, the more they emerge, the more emphatically they reveal that the basic pillars of the social order are deteriorating.[8]

Here we have this diffuse uneasiness brought together in a nutshell. Social authorities of the Kingdom in general, the best-informed of whom were the royal bureaucrats, were terribly alarmed at an apparently new tendency for people in the popular classes to place their own pleasures and needs above their obligations to the community. In religion, family life, allegiance to one's employer, in such diverse realms of public behavior as politics and dancing, and in such private realms of existence as sexuality, observers feared that old

7. *Ibid.*, 1836/1837 Amts-Inspektionen.
8. Printed in Georg Döllinger, *Sammlung der im Gebiete der inneren Staats-verwaltung des Königreichs Bayern bestehenden Verordnungen*, 33 vols. (Munich, 1835–1854), 26: 628. Verordnung of January 6, 1851.

community standards and ways were breaking down, and that personal emancipation—"egoistical" and dangerously "unbridled"—was leaping forth from the ruins.

Who Was behind All This Immorality?

Now, if these men believed that morality in all places and among all groups was decaying, we might dismiss their statements as neurotic ramblings. But the indictment was quite precise: women and young people. Groups most stricken with the virus of egoism were those which previously had been held most in thrall by various social hierarchies. Thus it was that in the Vormärz women, who previously had been in woefully subordinate positions within family authority structures, and youth, which as a group had been subject to the tightest community social controls, seemed to be in revolt.

Of course not all women and all youth. The official indictment cited especially those in dependent employment situations within the household and the traditional handicrafts.

As conservative social theorists have never ceased to complain, patriarchal employment relationships within the craft system surrendered between the mid-eighteenth and mid-nineteenth centuries to the impersonal "cash nexus." Traditionally, journeymen and apprentices were supposed to live in the homes of the master craftsmen, eat at their tables, and submit to the masters' censure of their off-hour activities. The master craftsman held in his hands not only the reins of economic power, but of social, moral, and political as well. The master craftman's domestic authority guaranteed that in every aspect of life the journeymen and apprentices would submit to the demands of a highly hierarchical family community. Early in the nineteenth century this web of association began to dissolve in Bavaria; the economic controls of master craftsman over journeyman were retained, the noneconomic variety lost. That is what all the shouting was about.

The municipal council of the city of Munich deplored in 1831 the havoc which the free market economy and state control had brought to the guild system. The "isolation" of individual producers and "the destruction of community co-operation" had led to the collapse of the moral principles of the earlier craft system. The state had abolished guild police powers in the "mistaken" assumption that all such powers were to devolve to the state itself. With the abolition of the morality controls which guilds and masters had earlier enjoyed came "wildness." "The journeyman knows no longer the domestic discipline of the master; he considers himself too adult for it and becomes less respectful. The apprentice follows the example of the journeyman." The younger masters too had ceased to heed the admonitions of their elders to work hard and to abstain from enjoying the pleasures of the moment.[9]

The shelves of petitions to the King and the government in Munich's state archives, the document volumes of the proceedings of the Lower Chamber of the legislature, the records of the provincial governments—all are virtually swimming in complaints from master craftsmen about the end of the guild system. Most of these complaints, to be sure, address overcompetition in the crafts through an excessively generous licensing policy, or official lenience in dealing with peddlers. But through many of them runs the scarlet thread of moral as well as economic collapse: young people simply refuse to assimilate the traditional corporative values of the craft system; they insist on going their individual ways, producing on their own hook, living outside the master's home, and, by taking on common-law wives or sleeping about

9. *Verhandlungen der Kammer der Abgeordneten des Königreichs Bayern*, 1831, VII Beilage Band, p. 61.

notoriously, scoffing at customary craft notions of honorableness.

Complaints about excessive independence among young workers extended to all master-servant relationships, and especially to domestic agricultural labor. Farm servants were, by the very nature of their employment, compelled to live in the farmer's house, but they manifested a sense of emancipation in ways which galled their employers just as much as journeymen outraged their masters. In 1820 the provincial government of Oberbayern lamented of rural servants: "All sense of what is just and proper is being lost. Each person is concerned only about momentary advantages, through whatever means. The dignity of the family bond, the discipline of the household, is disappearing." The reporter summed up this development in the word "Egoismus."[10] The Oberfranken government in the same year noted a tendency for servants to "escape all onerous tasks and to go over to a more comfortable existence."[11] In Mittelfranken the servants were said to evade domestic order and discipline.[12] Such laments had not abated by 1833, when in the triennial administrative reports the provincial governments were asked to comment on the "attitude and behavior of the serving classes." Oberbayern found a "decline in obedience"; the Oberpfalz noted a loosening of the bond between master and servant. And Unterfranken said: "The trend to a more independent life-style is predominant. . . ."[13] By 1848 provincial officials were reporting the almost complete disappearance of the earlier patriarchal relationships between rural master and servant.[14] It is important to keep in mind that the vast

10. MI 46546, May 23, 1820.
11. *Ibid.*, September 4, 1820.
12. *Ibid.*, October 11, 1820.
13. MI 15436.
14. See MI 46548, especially June 24, 1848, Mittelfranken to MI. Rolf Engelsing offers independent evidence of growing autonomy and indepen-

majority of these servants were young people, certainly less than thirty and often still in adolescence.

Many cultural critiques assigned to youth such a role in the general collapse of morality. The authority of parents over adolescent children seemed to be weakening. Young people now moved more freely, permitting themselves greater indifference to parental censure of their leisure-time activities. Augsburg's Dr. Koller was saddened to note in 1861 that in the good old days the paterfamilias would relax at home after a hard day's work in the small circle of children, servants, and journeymen which together comprised his "family." "But unfortunately that has almost completely stopped since such a variety of outside distractions are now offered even to this class of the population; therewith the bonds have loosened not only between master craftsman and journeyman, between employer and servant, but among the members of the smaller family circle as well." Even in a matter as innocuous as forms of address this loosening could be seen, for according to Dr. Koller, children had earlier addressed their parents with the respectful "Sie," at least among the upper strata of the social order. "In recent times relations have become much more familiar, and 'Du' is used almost everywhere."[15]

The Protestant and Catholic deputies to the Lower House presented in 1837 a joint petition in which they observed that both the raising of children and the supervision of servants was becoming more negligent. "It would not be exaggerated to say that in our days family life is dissolving." The custom in the "good old times" of spending one's nonworking hours in the family circle was becoming ever less fre-

---

dence among *Dienstboten* towards the end of the eighteenth century in his important article "Dienstbotenlektüre im 18. und 19. Jahrhundert in Deutschland," *International Review of Social History* 13 (1968): 384–429.

15. Bayerische Staatsbibliothek, Handschriftenabteilung, Cod. Ger. 6874 (10).

quent. The children were now exposed to adult entertainments. Indeed sophisticated amusements, whatever those were, were arranged for them.[16] When asked in 1833 to comment upon the province's morality, the Oberpfalz government summed things up: "The truth of the matter is that people in general are becoming more sentimental and increasing in self-esteem, while the simple old customs in domestic family life are vanishing." The youth had more "freedom of will," feared their elders less, reveled in irresponsibility, wantonness, "tearing-about," and mischief. The root of the evil was an "emancipation from all control, an exaggerated feeling of independence."[17] If these otherwise sober, responsible officials were right, we are dealing with a fundamental historical shift in the social position of youth. If they were wrong, we have before us merely the eternally constant conflict of generations.

A final group whom the Bavarian social authorities thought insurgent and individualistic were lower-class women, especially young women, and most particularly those in service. Whereas many other scholars have noted contemporary complaints about "the servant problem," few to my knowledge have detected an undercurrent of anxiety on the subject of women. Perhaps the silence of other historians on this subject is owing merely to a previous lack of interest in women's history; perhaps on the other hand I am attaching too much importance to a few casual remarks in the administrative correspondence, making of eternal male apprehensiveness about women a historical trend. Only further research, both in Bavaria and in other places, will clarify (a)

16. MI 46560, June 4, 1837. On the Catholic Church's attitude to morality questions, see recently Fintan Michael Phayer, *Religion und das Gewöhnliche Volk in Bayern in der Zeit von 1750–1850* (Munich, 1970; Neue Schriftenreihe des Stadtarchiv Münchens: Miscellanea Bavarica Monacensia, Heft 21).

17. MI 15396.

whether a new note of fearfulness on the position of women comes to characterize the social comment of the educated middle classes, and (b) whether the position of lower-class women was actually changing. My own conviction is that both questions must be answered affirmatively, but I emphasize the tentativeness of my argument on this subject.

In any event, a large number of references to a process one can only call female emancipation turn up in routine administrative correspondence on quite humdrum matters. Here is an example from Unterfranken's triennial administrative report for 1833: "One widespread and wellfounded complaint is that moral corruption is on the upswing, especially among female servants, who often spend the last cent of their wages upon gratifying their love of finery, their lust for pleasure; and when their wages (which have risen considerably) are exhausted, they not infrequently permit themselves to be led into wayward paths."[18] What these women were being emancipated from, however, was not necessarily men—as a later generation of female emancipators would attempt—but from a complex lattice of community power relationships and cultural rules calling for subservience. These lower-class women were steering increasingly towards asserting their self-worth as equal to that of women of any other social class. They were heading away from social roles of service, and from social controls enforcing modesty and chastity before marriage.

A hundred and fifty years later the scholar turns his ear close to the set, trying desperately to tune out the static of nostalgia, of envy of youth, and of masculine fantasies about female aggressiveness from the beat of historical change. His hand steadies on the dial at the bleatings and squawkings which social theories devised by other scholars for other times and places suggest might be present in Bavaria. And he

18. MI 15436.

is likely to brighten at the mention of "youth," "women," and "servants" because a host of hypotheses advanced by writers such as Gillis, Millett, Hobsbawm, and Rudé lead him to think that particular music might have played in Bavaria as well.[19] Yet the warning sign cannot be too clearly posted: world of the imagination, of men imagining women are changing, of older people imagining youth are more restless, of good burghers imagining in every gardener a Spartacus. The historian must be cautious indeed in taking this fantasy world as a mirror of reality.

Forms of Cultural Change: Luxury and Pleasure-Seeking

Just as certain groups of the population were selected in this cultural critique for harsh notice, certain forms of behavior were indicted as well. There are several areas of popular life in which stirrings of the private "wish to be free" leapt glaringly into the public eye, and these areas were seen by the bureaucrats as the very core of the cultural crisis. Clothing, alcohol, dancing, and sexuality all gave to the popular classes scope for the expression of self. In all, community morality could be explicitly renounced.

19. On the history of European adolescence see the 1971 circulated paper by John R. Gillis, "Youth and History: An Introduction." Kate Millett's *Sexual Politics* (New York, 1970) argues that militancy among emancipated middle-class women, at least, began in England early in the nineteenth century; Olwen Hufton's "Women in Revolution, 1789–1796," is silent on long-term changes, but describes active female participation in the Revolution. *Past and Present*, no. 53 (November, 1971): 90–108. On the insurgency of farm laborers under capitalist agriculture see Eric Hobsbawm and George Rudé, *Captain Swing* (New York, 1968), and Helmut Bleiber, *Zwischen Reform und Revolution: Lage und Kämpfe der schlesischen Bauern und Landarbeiter im Vormärz, 1840–1847* (East Berlin, 1966), pp. 57–81. None of these subjects—youth, women, or the serving classes in the nineteenth century—has ever to my knowledge received monographic treatment for Bavaria.

Clothing was, in the view of the Kingdom's officials, the most outward and visible sign of an inner moral disintegration. What exactly was changing? Joseph Hazzi, a royal bureaucrat, traveled through Altbaiern around 1800, making notes of social conditions. He was shocked by the lavishness of popular dress in many districts, especially in the prosperous county of Straubing. There everyone, above all the youth, indulged in finery: the farmers' sons wore beaver hats with gold braid, gold laces, and a silver clasp, red jerseys, light blue coats costing eight to twelve gulden per *Elle* (.83 meters), a green silk sash, a leather belt "of uncommon width" with various decorations and a silver buckle, two pocket watches with silver chains, black Lederhosen with ribbons, white and blue stockings made of cotton or silk (wool would have been customary), shoes with silver buckles, and silver rings.

The farmers' daughters appeared no less splendiferous: headscarves of the "finest" Swiss linen with Dutch lacework, silver clasps, precious scarves around their necks, red jackets of the "finest cloth costing ten to twelve gulden" with golden adornments, corsets of gold and silver material, white cotton stockings, silver chains, gold and silver rings, and so forth. Hazzi detailed the great value of every piece of apparel and was horrified by the expenditure involved. The cotters, laborers, and servants apparently imitated this dress to the extent that they could afford it.[20] This brief description conveys some idea what "luxury" in clothing meant to cultural critics. But while Hazzi deplored the expensive embellishment, he did not attack the Straubing dress as deviating from the traditional peasant costume.

Two decades later the lower classes, that is, people beneath the level of those whom Hazzi describes, began to

20. *Statistische Aufschlüsse über das Herzogthum Baiern . . .* , 11 vols. (Nürnberg, 1801–1808), 4: 144–145.

draw critical fire, not merely because their traditional clothing was expensive, but because they were beginning to *look*
like the upper classes. Johann von Pelkhoven, a parliamen-
tarian, complained about the "fondness of finery" seizing the
lower orders. "Is it still possible to tell the chambermaid from
the lady, the valet from the royal councilor, the counting-
house clerk from the banker?" Even the farmer, sighed Pelkhoven, had laid his simple jacket and breeches aside, putting
on instead the burgher's coat "with its metal buttons." The
farmer's pants and half-leather boots now made him appear
a bourgeois. The simple linen headbands of the "rustic beau-
ties" had given way to long decorated shawls. "A shorter
skirt, cut like chemise, places neither the full hips nor the
cute foot at a disadvantage, and white cotton stockings and
dyed leather shoes cause it to be forgotten that this particular
foot is mired in the filth of the stables during the week."[21]

These changes in style were branded "luxury," a term not
exclusively for clothing but bringing also under anathema
other such unseemly expenditures as brandy, tobacco, and
fine foods. Oerthel's *Dictionary of Foreign Words,* for example, defines "Luxus" as: "(1) a life of pleasure, luxury, de-
bauchery; (2) display of pomp, love of pomp, excessive expenditure on clothing, household goods, and entertainment;
(3) excessive growth of plants."[22]

The word's chief connotation, however, was that the lower
classes were dressing themselves with improper elegance.
The critics of lower-class clothing also employed other terms
like "Hoffahrt" (vaingloriousness) and "Kleiderpracht"
(splendiferous taste in clothing). But the word one encoun-
ters most frequently in the sartorial context is *Luxus.* "Luxury" along with its companion "pleasure-seeking" *(Genus-*

21. *Über das Gewerbe in Baiern* (Munich, 1818), pp. 95–96.
22. Ansbach, 1830, p. 572. I am grateful to Dr. Leonhard Link for this
reference.

sucht) represented the conventional diagnosis of the moral ailments of the lower orders.

Consider the baneful consequences of luxury in clothing. The Oberbayern government thought luxury, along with pleasure-seeking, the main factor in illegitimacy.[23] The Schwaben government in 1833 considered luxury the cause of skyrocketing wages for rural labor, and officials in the Oberpfalz thought *Luxus* in 1848 the chief source of the "demoralization" of the servant class.[24] A certain Weig, county clerk in Pfarrkirchen, assigned luxury as the cause of poverty in the Kingdom. "Many of the large farmers waste their money on expensive clothes and fabrics such as even a prosperous nobleman could not have contemplated in former times." The servants, he claimed, were even worse. But the cities were most corrupt of all: "In the cities and small towns sartorial magnificence has attained such heights that even day laborers, whose parents live in dire poverty, do not shun the finest cottons, flowers, hats, linen and silk garments, cut elegantly to the latest fashions, whereby vainglory and all other vices are much advanced, and other people, who hitherto had held themselves back, egged on to imitation."[25]

That was the heart of the matter. Weig, in his provincial outrage, had galloped across an important truth. Groups which previously had "held themselves back" were now participating in the blossoming of expressive behavior of which clothing was such a striking hallmark. New cultural forces were clearly moving across the face of popular life, changing most strongly those groups whom we have observed above.

"Pleasure-seeking" was the Siamese twin of luxury. And if *Luxus* meant the wearing of unseemly clothing, then "pleasure-seeking" meant indulging in entertainments which ear-

23. MI 52136, December 1, 1840.
24. MI 15436; MI 46548, July 12, 1848.
25. MH 9612, Preisausschreiben 33, December 30, 1848.

lier had seemed improper for the lower classes. Pleasure-seeking, like luxury, could cover a wide variety of human activities, all those in fact which might lead to "egoism" from social subordinates, making them less responsive to their masters and social superiors. Among such acts of self-indulgence were smoking tobacco, celebrating the "illegal" holidays, and "staying out late at night." But on the whole, critics of the lower classes meant by "pleasure-seeking" two particular activities: drinking and dancing.

Alcohol was thought a principal flag of surrender to selfish desires. Although there is no objective evidence that the density of taverns increased during the Vormärz (somewhat the opposite in fact), the consumption of beer was rising, and that of brandy appears to have been doing so as well.[26] The Oberfranken government was in 1833 able to declare a general decline in public drunkenness, yet noted that recently potato brandy had surpassed beer in popularity. Competition among distillers had depressed the price of hard liquor, causing both health and morality to decline.[27] A special royal commission, sent to investigate poverty in the Franconian town of Orb, analyzed popular drinking patterns thus: "Water is the general drink, beer an article of luxury for the well-to-do; but brandy is the magic potion that brings for a moment riches to the poor, joy to the sorrowful, health to the ailing, sleep to the children, and lets all forget their hunger. Brandy accompanies the poor of Orb from the cradle to the grave. The dying man enjoys his last pleasure with brandy, and dies in the euphoria of intoxication, just as his mother, in

26. I have calculated tavern densities over time in "Social Change and Social Policy in Bavaria, 1800–1860" (Ph.D. diss., Harvard University, 1967), pp. 463–464. Average beer consumption per head in Bavaria rose from 1.15 hectoliters in 1807–1808 to 1.60 hl. in 1858–1859. Emil Struve, *Die Entwicklung des Bayerischen Braugewerbes in neunzehnten Jahrhundert* (Leipzig, 1893), p. 65.

27. MI 15394.

a similar condition, had brought him into the world."[28]

Policymakers thought dire consequences to result from an increased consumption of alcohol. For one thing, if the lower classes spent all their money on liquor, they would become public charges, or else be unable to work because they were intoxicated.[29] Those officials more attuned to the economy, such as Joseph Hazzi, laid a neglect of work to tavern frequentation. Of Griesbach County: "The daily routine of a local farmer consists of attending early mass after awakening, then going to the tavern where he eats meat and drinks brandy; thereupon he works about his fields a bit until noon; after eating he goes again to the tavern, and remains there until around nine o'clock in the evening, playing cards for often quite high stakes. Drunkenness is for this reason not infrequent, nor is intemperance in love."[30] Munich's episcopal chancellery claimed in 1854 that drinking incited rebellious spirits: in the tavern young people felt themselves on home ground where they need pay less attention to religion, morality, and order.[31] And the Interior Ministry noted with concern an article in the *Nürnberger Estaffete* in 1835, which complained that "young fellows are found until late at night smoking and drinking in the taverns and other public places."[32]

The Interior Ministry was scandalized by the "dying sister story," which captures as though in marble the anxiety of these social critics about youth and alcohol. The *Bamberger Regierungsblatt* reported the following incident: "How far

28. MI 58366, May 11, 1835.

29. For a typical complaint see the report on poverty in the Gemeinde of Wolfsmünster (Unterfranken), MI 59432, January 19, 1841.

30. *Statistische Aufschlüsse*, 3: 1130.

31. *Generalien-Sammlung der Erzdiozese München und Freising. Die oberhirtlichen Verordnungen und allgemeinen Erlässe von 1821 bis 1846*, 3 vols. (Munich, 1847–1848), 2: 491.

32. MI 46560, August 14, 1835.

the demoralization of the lower classes has progressed is seen in the following incident in a nearby village. A young man who was sitting in the tavern was called by his mother to the bedside of his dying sister. He however replied: 'You run ahead and tell her to wait until I've finished my beer.' "[33]

If this increased alcohol consumption pointed to a rise in alcoholism, that would square ill with the argument about cultural change I present in these pages, indicating sooner a search for relief from desperation. But I believe that more drinking was simply the consequence of more sociability: people were going out more, intent upon having a good time; they naturally ended up in the tavern, and drank.

Just as in the realms of clothing and alcohol, a genuine shift in popular dancing customs appears to have taken place in the years 1800–1860. The traditional, sedate folk dances were dying out in Bavaria, giving way to more active styles of dancing. Friedrich Karl, Graf von Giech, noted in a commentary on the Kingdom's public life written just after his retirement as provincial governor of Mittelfranken, the transformation of popular dancing: "how everything region-alistic and ethnic is becoming increasingly watered-down and empty, how people entertain themselves with graceless, clumsy imitations of the dances of the upper classes. . . ."[34] By the mid-1840s the amusements of the Viennese romantics had reached the Franconian countryside.

New dancing styles were jouncing, jostling, and sensuous. Listen to the local doctor describe the waltzes, gallopades, and polkas of Altdorf County around 1859. Often a few farm lands would start things off with a song; then music by the

33. *Ibid.*, attached to letter of January 18, 1835; I have already recounted this anecdote in "Sexual Change and Illegitimacy: The European Experience," in *Modern European Social History*, ed. Robert J. Bezucha (Lexington, Mass., 1972), pp. 231–269.

34. *Ansichten über Staats- und öffentliches Leben* (Nürnberg, 1843), pp. 92–93.

band and dancing to the accompaniment of loud shouting would follow. "In general a terrible stamping of the feet takes place in such festivities, an incessant howling, whistling, singing, and horselike neighing, so that the music of the clarinets and trumpets is drowned out. Remaining for any time among these exuberant, joyous youths, even if no old fogy, is simply impossible." The good doctor noted that during intermission all participants ate and drank "heartily," mostly beer and coffee; he concluded his account by calling dances "the seedbeds of illegitimate births."[35]

Dancing was, as the Altdorf doctor pointed out, virtually the only popular amusement in many parts of the Kingdom. A good indicator of dancing's real importance to the common man is the hostility with which efforts to limit it were greeted. The priest in a small hamlet near Pfronten (Schwaben), for example, had learned of a house in which dancing was going on "in secret." The following Sunday he condemned all such entertainment from his pulpit, comparing dancing to that order of events which had generated the Flood in biblical times. He warned "all honorable men not to enter such a house." This action, the priest confessed, turned out to have been a blunder for the enraged dancers tried later to drive him from the parish.[36] In 1849 the Constitutional and Craft Society in Windsheim (Mittelfranken) petitioned the king to repeal the government decree of 1843 which had limited dancing. The petition spoke of "oppressive tutelage" and "personal freedom." Had dancing played only a minor role in popular life, this would have been strong language indeed for such a bagatelle.[37] During the Revolution of 1848 the Mittelfranken government itself empha-

---

35. Bayerische Staatsbibliothek, Handschriftenabteilung, Cod. Germ. 6874 (2), Beilage 2.

36. Magnus Jocham, *Memoiren eines Obskuranten. Eine Selbstbiographie*, ed. P. Magnus Sattler (Kempten, 1896), pp. 377–378.

37. MH 6143, sometime in March, 1849.

sized popular resentment of the 1843 decree as a cause of popular discontent.[38] So we are dealing here with a sphere of popular life more important than would appear at first glance.

What, then, were these dances like? How often did they take place? The episcopal chancellery of the archdiocese of Munich-Freising gives us a statistical overview of the number of dances in the archdiocese for the year 1852. In the 354 parishes of the archdiocese, excluding the cities of Munich and Landshut, 4,842 dances took place in around 1,200 taverns and 860 villages. Of these 4,842, 1,533 were occasioned by saint's day festivals, 1,490 by marriage celebrations, 330 by annual guild celebrations, and 1,489 by "various occasions." The latter category included 148 social balls and approximately the same number of celebrations at annual market fairs. Thus an average of 134 dances took place in each of the archdiocese's 36 deaneries, and an average of 13 per year in each parish, excluding saint's day festivals, marriage celebrations, and occasional concerts (these are the archdiocese's calculations).[39] If people wanted to go dancing, then, they did not lack opportunity.

The episcopal chancellery considered average participation at these dances high. Counting both those entitled to dance as members of the private party or the local community, and those unentitled but present, the office estimated a normal dance as having about forty participants. On days when many communities arranged such festivities, dances were so pervasive that no one in the archdiocese would have to travel more than an hour or two in order to reach a dancing site.

The duration of the festivities seemed overlong, to the archdiocese. On workdays the dancing would normally start

38. MI 45786, October 29, 1849.
39. *Generalien-Sammlung*, 2: 490.

around noon; on holidays, after the end of church services. Things were supposed to stop at curfew hour, in rural communities from nine to ten at night, in towns from ten to eleven o'clock, depending upon the season. But the local compilers of these statistics noted many dances which lasted well into the night, official permission to extend them having been obtained. And even after the dancing had stopped, the drinking often continued until dawn, "not infrequently with noise and song." All this was much worse in Munich, where more and longer dances took place. "The abuse still continues that lawn parties diminish the ranks of the early-morning churchgoers."[40]

If Freiherr von Giech and the local doctor in Altdorf, to cite two of many observers, were right, this pattern of widespread dancing we have observed for the 1850s was a recent development. And the styles of dancing too had probably evolved markedly from the eighteenth century. It is most difficult to pin down changes over time in something like dancing with reliable quantitative data. Should serial statistics exist on the sheer frequency of popular concerts and dances, they might reflect changes in the level of government control rather than changes in popular sociability. I can venture only the weak quantitative assessment that in a perusal of some administrative correspondence for the late eighteenth century—the sort of vein in which such nuggets as references to dancing would be likely to appear—I have met only silence. Either dancing was of reduced importance at this point in time, or government administrators were not alarmed about it. My highly intuitive impression is that only in the 1820s do references to dancing become both commonplace and fearful, suggesting perhaps a change in the frequency and form of this important dimension of popular culture.

40. *Ibid.*, pp. 491–492.

Change in Sexual Behavior

At the very core of *la vie intime* lies sexuality, the intersection of basic personal needs and popular cultural patterns. Contemporary observers feared the former was changing—that people were becoming more sexualized, more avid for erotic gratification, more willing to overthrow prudent social safeguards for private pleasure. My own view is that the latter element—the cultural matrix within which a number of sexual roles are embedded—was in transformation, and that new operating procedures for courtship were being worked out. Changes in these cultural rules reflected sooner a shift in the nature of marriage and in the individual's relationship to community authority than it did a deepening of the "sex drive."[41]

Dancing gives us an entry point to the world of popular sexuality. Contemporaries spotted a variety of interconnections, and we have no reason to question their perceptions. One cultural rule suggested (perhaps dictated is too strong) that later in the evening sexual intercourse would follow dancing. In Oberbayern, for example, it was customary for women to appear unescorted at dance locales, and wait until they had been asked to dance or had found a male partner to escort them home. It was claimed that the walk home customarily involved a stop-off for sexual intercourse.[42] Joseph Hazzi observed a further refinement of this custom (his outrage suggests he believed it to have been an innovation): "The girl is happy when her suitor buys her a beer [at a

41. Among recent work emphasizing the cultural context of sexual behavior, see "Psychosexual Development," in *The Sexual Scene*, eds. William Simon and John H. Gagnon (New York, 1970), pp. 23–41; Michael Schofield, *The Sexual Behaviour of Young People* (Harmondsworth, England, Pelican edition, 1968).

42. MI 46556, February 22, 1837.

dance], for that is the chief advertisement of romance. Therefore the man who is identified as the father [of an illegitimate child] usually says, if he can or wants to get out of it: 'I didn't buy you any beer.' "[43]

Thus did pregnancy and illegitimacy result from dancing. The province of Mittelfranken claimed that four-fifths of all paternity suits arose from the saint's day festivals. In the "gay city" of Weissenburg "people dance from Pentecost until the middle of October every Monday in the wine cellars. Thus does it happen that Weissenburg County has a great number of illegitimate children and couples living in sin, of which thirteen were officially disbanded in a single year."[44]

Did the sexual behavior of young people in Bavaria change in the period 1800 to 1860? This is the most difficult evidential problem of all, for complaints from the middle-aged that the younger generation is more sexualized seem virtually a historical constant. And if independent documentation did not exist, confirming these bureaucratic lamentations about increased intercourse, one would be reluctant indeed to give them much weight.

Observers reasoned backwards from illegitimacy to sexuality. Because, as we shall see in a moment, the incidence of illegitimacy was soaring, they believed levels of premarital intercourse to have been going up as well. Hazzi, for example, was able to discover few virgins in Oberbayern, although his investigative techniques may have lacked in clinical precision. In the area around Seefeld he reported both sexes to be "so fond of sensual pleasure that scarcely a girl under twenty is to be found who is not already a mother." Around Marquartstein this enjoyment of sex was part of a spirit of independence. There the proverb "We'll have no masters" was popular among people who married "eagerly and very

43. *Statistische Aufschlüsse*, 3: 1131–1132; Landgericht Griesbach.
44. MI 15394, 1833.

early, and who had many children, among them so many illegitimate ones that this was not considered sinful but instead a good work."[45] Oberfranken testified in 1833 that communities full of deflowered maidens were commonplace. "In the countryside a girl who has preserved her virgin purity until age 20 is exceptional, and moreover is scarcely lauded among her peers for this accomplishment."[46] In Unterfranken even the landholding classes, as well as urban laborers, had by 1839 concluded that "the natural satisfaction of the sex drive is neither legally forbidden nor morally sinful."[47] Another sign of the times was in applications for marriage licenses, whereby it had become customary for officials to ask if illegitimate children were present.[48]

In 1854 premarital sex had apparently become so commonplace that Oberbayern reported hysterically (citing statements from county officials): "any meeting between single youths and girls, for dancing or other public entertainment, ends with fornication; in places where male and female servants work next to each other that sexual intercourse is a daily happening, and the County of Altötting observes that having had children before marriage is not thought shameful at all."[49]

Perhaps each generation does believe that it is the last before the Flood, yet I have seen nothing in the administrative correspondence of the late eighteenth or early nineteenth century to compare with these perceptions of sinfulness of the 1840s and 50s. Had the fantasy life of these otherwise sober, matter-of-fact administrators suddenly spilled into their official papers, or was sexual behavior really changing?

45. *Statistische Aufschlüsse*, 3: 193, 657.
46. MI 15396.
47. MI 46556, February 30, 1839.
48. *Ibid.*, February 22, 1837.
49. MI 52137, February 12, 1854.

The evidence of illegitimacy says that these statements, though perhaps a trifle overwrought, were fundamentally right. Illegitimacy rose substantially from the middle of the eighteenth century to late in the 1860s, when the repressive legislation against the marriage of the poor was repealed. Although national figures are not available before 1825, several local studies demonstrate a low illegitimacy ratio for the eighteenth century: between 5 and 10 percent of all births illegitimate.[50] By the nineteenth century this ratio had increased markedly, reaching a high point of 24 percent in 1859–1860.[51]

But if the illegitimacy ratio moves, many factors other than increased sexual activity could be responsible, such as variations in the tendency of pregnant women to marry before the child's birth, changes in contraceptive practice, indeed shifts in the level of legitimate fertility or in the number of unmarried women in the population.

So without further argumentation we cannot conclude that an increase in the illegitimacy ratio confirms the gloomy diagnoses of Bavaria's royal bureaucracy. An alternative measure of the tendency of young people to have sex before marriage is the prebridal pregnancy rate, which is to say, the percent of first children born within eight months of marriage. An increase in bridal pregnancy means almost certainly that an increasing percentage of couples has become sexually active before marriage (unless the illegitimate fer-

50. Stephan Glonner, "Bevölkerungs-Bewegung von sieben Pfarreien im Kgl. Bayerischen Bezirksamte Tölz seit Ende des XVI. Jahrhunderts," *Allgemeines Statistisches Archiv* 4 (1896): 263–279; Michael Phayer kindly made available to me illegitimacy data he had collected for 16 Oberbayern villages in the period 1760–1825; Ludwig Schmidt-Kehl, "Wandel im Erb- und Rassengefüge zweier Rhönorte, 1700–1936," *Archiv für Bevölkerungswissenschaft* 7 (1937): 176–199.

51. Friedrich Lindner, *Die unehelichen Geburten als Sozialphänomen: Ein Beitrag zur Statistik der Bevölkerungsbewegung im Königreiche Bayern* (Leipzig, 1900), p. 217.

tility rate were simultaneously to drop, which would mean that couples who previously had stayed unmarried until after a bastard's birth were now getting married before the birth). Prebridal pregnancy data are difficult to accumulate, because they involve family reconstitution, a painstaking linking of records from parish registers of baptism, marriage, and death. But the two family reconstitutions already done for Bavaria show a pronounced rise in prenuptial conception between the middle of the eighteenth and the middle of the nineteenth centuries. In Anhausen (Schwaben) the percentage of all brides who gave birth within eight and a half months after marriage rose from 14 percent in 1692–1749 to 20 percent in 1800–1849. And in Kreuth (Oberbayern) bridal pregnancy claimed from 3 percent in 1740–1799 to a staggering 29 percent in 1800–1839.[52] This increase in bridal pregnancy, combined with the rise in the illegitimacy ratio, suggests that sexual activity before marriage was definitely increasing in the period 1760–1860. If these sample results continue to hold up for other communes in the Kingdom, the bureaucrats who saw Sodom and Gomorrah rising again in the fertile plains of Niederbayern and the upland slopes of Oberfranken will probably have been right.

Completing the Argument

Let us assume for the sake of an argument that the popular classes in Bavaria, especially young people and women, decisively changed their minds in the first half of the nineteenth century about the balance of allegiance they were willing to strike between personal emancipation and community obligation. Let us assume that this change of view among hun-

52. John Knodel, "Two and a Half Centuries of Demographic History in a Bavarian Village," [Anhausen] *Population Studies* 24 (1970): 353–376; Jacques Houdaille, "Quelques résultats sur la démographie de trois villages d'Allemagne de 1750 à 1879," *Population* 25 (1970): 649–654.

dreds of thousands of anonymous people was part of a larger historical movement away from subordination to community hierarchy and towards individual autonomy. Let us finally assume that these bureaucratic observers, who themselves were so close to the fabric of popular life without actually being part of it, were substantially correct in their analyses of a "moral crisis." Readers who for a moment are willing to suspend disbelief at this case, one illustrated but not proven, may wish to consider in conclusion two general points.

First, this fundamental transformation of *la vie intime* seems to have taken place in many other parts of Europe as well between the mid-eighteenth and mid-nineteenth centuries. Readers possessing even a passing familiarity with, say, the polemical literature of eighteenth-century England, or the principal social analyses of early nineteenth-century France, will recall at once the shrieks of moral outrage against "impudence," "libertine comportment," "social ambitiousness," or "unseemly finery."[53] This outpouring of resentment and fear was widespread, but not universal for in some places complaints about the lower orders remained in modulation, at the level of a historical constant; nostalgia and fear of loss will in all times and all countries produce a certain background rumbling of morality complaints. In southern France there seems to have been only faint echoes of such complaints (although we are reading uncertain seismographs), and in the publicistic literature of southern Italy during the late eighteenth and early nineteenth centuries

53. Among many writings on England, see D. E. C. Eversley, "The Home Market and Economic Growth in England, 1750–1780," in *Land, Labour, and Population in the Industrial Revolution: Essays Presented to J. D. Chambers*, eds. E. L. Jones and G. E. Mingay (London, 1967), pp. 206–259, esp. p. 212. The subject has been less studied in France, but recently, with emphasis on the Church's attitudes, see "The Conflict of Moralities: Confession, Sin, and Pleasure in the Nineteenth Century," in *Conflicts in French Society*, ed. Theodore Zeldin (London, 1970), pp. 13–50.

the presentiment of morality crisis is barely audible in the background, the foreground of public consciousness dominated by entirely different crashes and shouts.[54] It is in those parts of Europe undergoing rapid modernization, involving the spread of cottage industry or the construction of central-state administrations, that complaints about a morality crisis rise to this piercing, all-pervasive screech. Northern Europe, Western Europe, and the British Isles are the sites of lamentation about popular morality, and these are the regions where precisely that variety of social change that weakened the authority of traditional social controls, and instilled in individuals a new sense of self, was proceeding apace.

Consider the one realm of *la vie intime* subject to quantitative analysis: illegitimacy and prebridal pregnancy. All over Europe illegitimacy ratios were shooting upwards, and levels of "shotgun weddings" were rising as well. I have elsewhere argued that increased sexual activity among young people was responsible for this jump in out-of-wedlock conceptions, and reached this conclusion with information much more complete than that for Bavaria.[55]

Similarly, all over Europe the consumption of alcohol was

54. Only a careful historical investigation, making explicit comparisons among these societies will sustain this generalization. Yet if morality complaints had risen above a whisper in lower Provence, for example, one would have expected one of Maurice Agulhon's magisterial works to have picked them up. *Pénitents et francs-maçons de l'ancienne Provence* (Paris, 1968); *La Vie sociale en Provence intérieure au lendemain de la Révolution* (Paris, 1970); or *La République au village* (Paris, 1970). What I have been able to learn—unsystematic and incomplete though these hesitant researches have been—about the polemical literature in other such "backward" corners of Europe as northern Sweden or southern Italy suggests that "moral collapse" took a relatively low ranking in the list of things people felt were wrong with their society. Yet I am aware of the dangers in the argument of silence, and venture this cross-national comparison with the utmost tentativeness.

55. Edward Shorter, "Illegitimacy, Sexual Revolution, and Social Change in Modern Europe," *Journal of Interdisciplinary History* 2 (1971): 237–272, reviews available statistics on illegitimacy between 1750 and 1850.

rising in the nineteenth century; new patterns of popular entertainment were evolving; and new styles of family life began to spring forth that meant more personal autonomy for all concerned.[56]

The first point, then, is that Bavaria fits into a wider European pattern, rather than being an isolated region with an idiosyncratic development. Whatever the cause of the phenomenon, the process of cultural change itself reached out to embrace millions of people from Wales to Kärnten.

The second point is that contemporary analyses of a "moral crisis" were only half-right. Egoism was in fact at work, and traditional community controls upon individuals were in fact breaking down. But "the wish to be free," as Fred Weinstein and Gerald Platt have observed, did not spring merely from a removal of external controls upon personal passions.[57] The geyser-like explosion was not just the result of removing the lid of custom. Respect for authority was an *internalized* value among most of Europe's lower orders, and to explain why that respect gave way to more "egoistic" emotions one must explain why a new value system came to replace an old

56. Among the literature on alcoholism and alcohol consumption see Brian Harrison, *Drink and the Victorians: The Temperance Question in England, 1815–1872* (London, 1971). William Langer, citing Irish and Swedish data, speaks of the Vormärz as the "golden age of inebriation." *Political and Social Upheaval, 1832–1852* (New York, 1969), p. 14. On changes in patterns of leisure time, see Joffre Dumazedier's speculations in *Vers une civilisation du loisir?* (Paris, 1962). And for specific instances of new recreations among factory workers in the nineteenth century, Georges Duveau, *La Vie ouvrière en France sous le Second Empire*, 2d ed. (Paris, 1946), p. 467. Finally, on changes in family life under the impact of industrialization, see Rudolf Braun, *Industrialisierung und Volksleben: Die Veränderungen der Lebensformen in einem ländlichen Industriegebiet vor 1800 (Zürcher Oberland)* (Erlenbach-Zürich, 1960); and Neil J. Smelser, *Social Change in the Industrial Revolution: An Application of Theory to the British Cotton Industry, 1770–1840* (Chicago, 1959).

57. Fred Weinstein and Gerald M. Platt, *The Wish to be Free: Society, Psyche, and Value Change* (Berkeley, 1969).

one. There was to be sure a dissolution of traditional cultural patterns, but no normative void. The new values of individual self-expression and self-development that the popular classes started to internalize between 1750 and 1850 were learned from a new culture. Or perhaps, these values were learned as part of a freshly-arisen, lower-class subculture, for among the middle classes old belief systems persisted long past the beginning of the nineteenth century.

The point is that what contemporaries perceived as a breakdown was just a switch, a replacement of one set of cultural operating rules with another. There was no normlessness, no value confusion, no running off the rails in matters that occupy us here (if, in fact, anywhere). But the bureaucratic observers we have been listening to in this paper, at least, disliked the content of the new rules, and refused to believe that they existed at all.

Why this new subculture spread is a major historical problem, an agenda for future research in both Bavaria and other parts of Europe where "morality" seemed to be threatened.

Of Time, Work, and Leisure

SEBASTIAN DE GRAZIA

Thus far we have been looking at origins: the articles by Plumb and Shorter examine particular threads which were to weave together, over the course of the nineteenth century, in order to make up the fabric of leisure as we have defined it in the Introduction. Sebastian de Grazia is a distinguished American political scientist and philosopher who has written a brilliant book on the subject of leisure (which, incidently, he defines somewhat differently than we have chosen to do in this volume). In the following selection from this book de Grazia surveys the problem in a wide historical perspective. His analysis begins with the impact of the new work rhythms of industrial capitalism in England and extends through to a discussion of the impact of modern advertising, which has reached its greatest level of sophisti-

SOURCE: Sebastian de Grazia, *Of Time, Work, and Leisure* (Garden City, N. Y.: Doubleday Anchor Books, 1964) pp. 181–206. Copyright © 1962 by The Twentieth Century Fund, New York. Reprinted by permission of The Twentieth Century Fund.

cation in contemporary America. Looking at the kinds of changes which have occurred in the past 150 years or so, de Grazia draws some important connections between time, work, and leisure (the title of his work) which have not occurred to other students of the problem.

"The leisure problem," as it is called today, has existed ever since the beginning of Europe's transition from an agricultural and village world to an industrial society. Any uprooting of people will change things so much that time disappears in the flurry of reorientation to a strange world. Rather than explain everything, though, with an airy wave of the hand and a bored repetition of "The Industrial Revolution, of course," I propose to examine the reorientation more closely. In England its stages are clear. England's experience is valuable not simply because it was the first along the path, but also because that experience is close to ours. We share language and ancestors; in both of us the making of farmers and villagers into workers and the lack of an urban tradition have affected the case. For a half-century we followed this experience closely, tagging behind at times, stepping ahead at others. Since the turn of the present century the roles have been reversed. We now step ahead more than we tag behind.[1]

1. Among the works on English social and economic history of the nineteenth century, see John L. and Barbara Hammond, *The Bleak Age* (London: Longmans, 1934); and *The Town Labourer, 1760–1832* (London: Longmans, 1920); T. C. Barker and J. R. Harris, *A Merseyside Town in the Industrial Revolution: St. Helens, 1750–1900* (Liverpool: University Press, 1954); Charles Booth, ed., *Life and Labour of the People in London* (New York: Macmillan, 1892–1897); T. H. S. Escott, *England: Her People, Polity, and Pursuits* (New York: Holt, 1880); Guy Chapman, *Culture and Survival* (London: Cape, 1940); C. F. G. Masterman, *The Condition of England* (London, 1909); Henry Mayhew, *London Characters* (London: Chatton, 1881); G. M. Young, ed., *Early Victorian England, 1830–1865*, 2 vols. (1934); R. Nettel, *Seven Centuries of Popular Song* (London: Phoenix, 1956); W. H. Hutt, "The Factory System of the Early Nineteenth Century," and T. S.

The point at which we can begin is at the start of the fight over shorter hours. The movement took place between 1830 and 1850. From the time the Ten Hour Bill was enacted in 1847, free time instead of spare time can be said to have come fully to life in our age, and the modern problem of leisure was born with it. But the terms free time and leisure were not yet in great use. Idleness and drink were their precursors. The Ten Hour struggle was on the face of it a struggle for shorter hours, but as sometimes happens the face of it was not the heart of it. Often, as we shall mention again, the campaign of labor unions for a shorter workweek seems to be a tactic to distribute available jobs. The machines are ever doing the work of more men. If the work isn't spread, some or many men will be out of a job. The aim is protection rather than more free time. The same motive, it is clear, started the ball rolling for the first campaign for shorter hours in modern times, over 100 years ago.

On the surface the workers, primarily in the textile industries, were battling for shorter hours for women and children. Since over half the employees in textile factories were women, with adult men making up only a quarter and children the rest, it was unavoidable that if women and children had to be put on shorter hours, then everyone had to be put on shorter time. Otherwise, and this was the objective, only

---

Ashton, "The Standard of Life of the Workers in England 1790–1830," in *Capitalism and the Historians*, Friedrich A. von Hayek, ed. (Chicago: University of Chicago Press, 1954). For a picture at the end of the Middle Ages of English town life with its "townfields," George M. Trevelyan, *English Social History* (London: Longmans, 1946).

The new concern of the overdeveloped with the underdeveloped countries reveals that much of the English experience in industrialization is being repeated in the unmodern parts of the modern world. See Bert F. Hoselitz, "The City, the Factory, and Economic Growth," *American Economic Review* (May 1955); Simon Marcson, "Social Change and Social Structure in Transitional Societies," *International Journal of Comparative Sociology* (September 1960); and Wilbert E. Moore, *Industrialization and Labor* (Ithaca, N.Y.: Cornell University Press, 1951).

men could be employed—if machines with increasing horse-power could keep running long hours. If the surplus of adult male labor were drawn in, wage rates would also go up. From various sources it is clear, too, that the interest in children and women was secondary: at one bargaining stage the adult workers were willing to extend children's hours from nine to ten provided they could have a ten-hour day themselves. It need not be supposed the workers were deliberately con-cealing their motives. An early resolution of theirs minced no words: it was to equalize and extend labor by bringing into employment the many adult males who, though willing and ready to work, were obliged to spend their time in idleness, while females and children were compelled to labor ten to sixteen hours a day. The last part of the statement was taken up by persons outside of the working class and added to the list of brute facts about child labor in unhealthy and cruel surroundings. It thus became part of the humanitarian revolt that began to have an impact on Parliament. Before long, in about ten or fifteen years, the workingmen's reasons for con-tinuing this struggle had changed. Child labor receded far-ther into the background, young persons and women be-came the humane objective, but the shorter working day began to interest the workers in itself. Just before midcen-tury 70 percent of the men interviewed by the factory in-spector were in favor of the ten-hour day. Even many of those working twelve hours a day said they would prefer ten hours at less wages. The story begins to have more interest for us at this point.

Why does more time mean so much to them at this junc-ture, actually just when the final Ten Hour Bill was being drafted? Conditions were good, for one thing. The cost of living was going down, trade was active, piece rates had risen, new machines gave them more money in shorter time. A family at work was earning what it needed in much less time than the 11½-hour day. Now what do I mean when I say a family earned enough for what was needed? I refer here to what the families themselves thought they needed. For instance the bricklayers of those days set their wage rates themselves in each district by calculating the prices of food, house rent, and other things necessary for their subsistence. They appeared contented, said the secretary of their Society, with wages that pay for "the cost of living and a little more."[2] A cotton-mill worker reported cheerfully that with ten instead of twelve hours a man could do with one less meal a day and so save the money lost. The remark recalls the attitude of the Afghans; they have refused to work for the higher wages of industry because it means they will have to eat more. If the basic diet is oatmeal, herring, and potatoes, or bread, bacon, and tea, why not improve the diet? Certainly the Englishman or American today would consider the diet below not only the decent level but the nutrition level. Why choose time rather than food or other things?

To answer we have to go further back for a moment to see in the first place how the workers got to where they were, to wit, in the factories. England of the 1830s was on the verge of a transformation. It had already appeared in the textile industry but even there hand-loom weavers still competed with power-driven machinery. The country was standing on the edge between agrarianism and industry. The past still had a strong grip. Indeed it was the past, the then not so distant past, that was calling them back out of the factories. They or their children had at the end of the previous century just been uprooted by the enclosure movement and driven off the land. The hamlet no longer had a place for them, yet not until driven out would they leave. As far back as Elizabethan days, to supply the labor needed for industries newly expanded into the large-scale class—metallurgy, refineries,

2. The remark on "the cost of living and a little more" appears in Chapman, *Culture and Survival*.

shipbuilding—skilled workmen had to be imported from other countries, while unskilled English hands could be got only from forced labor, or by impressing rogues and rascally vagabonds, or by conditionally pardoning criminals and war prisoners.

Great forces held back the movement of labor. Workers had first to be removed, and gradually removed they were. When monastic lands were thrown on the market, sold, or presented to supporters by the king, the final owners in the last speculation that followed paid prices too high for any rent obtainable from tenants. To get a return on capital many owners laid down arable fields to grass for sheep, since wool was the backbone of the export trade. Tenant farmers, not being sheep, could not graze or yield wool. They were turned out and sheep brought in. The evicted had either to find new land in the waste marshes, moors, or forests, or go into service. In either case it meant a deserted hamlet and an uprooted people roaming the countryside. Vagrancy did not appeal to the Crown because it signified discontent and problems of law and order. It did not appeal to the farming landowners either, since it meant a shortage of seasonal labor. Lastly the towns with their guild hierarchies did not like the arrival of strangers in any number who might in the end, as in fact they did, disturb the balance of things. In the seventeenth century the Act of Settlement still tried to control vagrancy by impeding movement, thus contravening the desires of employers who cried a labor shortage.

The opening of the nineteenth century saw a phenomenal increase in population (about 18 percent from 1810 to 1820) due largely to the decrease in the death rate. From 1700 to 1750 the growth was 400,000; from 1750 to 1800 about 2½ million; after that, the rate of population increase rose even higher. This might appear to have been no problem to a modern employer seeking a labor supply; here it is a godsend. But it was like pulling a molar barehanded to get the villager out of his home. The spread of the enclosure system in the second half of the eighteenth century put an end to pioneering the wasteland; the frontier was now closed. Still the villager refused to submit. If he moved to find work, it was often to the nearest village, where if anything happened to him back he went to his parish, his last refuge. If he went too far out and stayed away he might lose the chance of the poorhouse. Even when a model employer or factory appeared on the scene to offer help to villagers near starvation, as rarely occurred, they chose their customary state. They might go with all their children to the factory with higher wages and steadier employment and get installed in the comfortable quarters provided them, but after a few weeks the going was too much.

Though they might be weavers and the factory a spinning mill, the new work habits required of them went against the grain. They returned to their bit of land, rented or owned, which they worked long in the summer, short in the winter. From their land they would move over to the stocking frames in their houses, then back to the land, and over to the frames again, with women and children doing their share. Here there was no having to stay with the unfeeling machine until someone shut off the power. The life they knew was unpunctual and chatty. A shoemaker got up in the morning when he liked and began work when he liked. If anything of interest happened, out he went from his stool to take a look himself. If he spent too much time at the alehouse drinking and gossiping one day, he made up for it by working till midnight the next. Like the Lapons or the Trobriand Islanders he worked by enthusiastic spurts and spent long periods without toil, which among nonindustrial communities is a way of working more common than is generally supposed. He made up his work with a willingness born of the fact that the backlog was of his own doing.

Then came the new Poor Law (1826) and Amendment

(1834) and finally the Union Chargeability Act (1865). The parish was pulled from under a man. If the parish could not help him keep his children from starving, a man was driven to work or to let his children out to industry. As factory workers these early employees left much for the employer to desire. The rural mentality was always with them. Up into the eighteenth century, mill owners had turned the men out to do field work whenever business was slack. Others had closed the mills in harvest and haymaking seasons and put their workers in the fields. Once the worker had earned enough, he quit. In the factory where piece rates were in effect, at the precise inch of cloth he stopped; in the mines, at the necessary pound of coal. A manufacturer trying to increase output, or merely count on regular production—it was enough to make him tear his hair. What he might have predicted was the worker's willingness to earn enough to buy his rock-bottom oatmeal, herring, and potatoes. Even this hunger was not absolute. Without any knowledge of calories, the worker knew that if he worked less, he earned less, sure, but he ate less too.

The new entrepreneurs, as they themselves wailed, seemed destined for bankruptcy. Laments over idleness perhaps hit their highest note in the first half of the nineteenth century. In the textile mills work had got more and more disagreeable because the new machines required the worker's unflagging punctuality and attention. First the four-, then the six-loom weaver made its bow to workers. Machines in the meantime had speeded up. The average number of picks woven per minute climbed steadily from ninety to 112 to 130. These and other improvements in but a few decades raised the earnings of the piece-rate workers, who, after all, comprised four-fifths of the industry. Of course this simply meant that they knocked off or wanted to knock off earlier. In areas, too, where mechanization was not notable the workers stopped working when enough was enough. The stonemasons of Newcastle, 422 strong in 1867, struck for shorter hours. Employers offered a pay raise if they would stay at work for the old hours. Four hundred and one of the men voted for the shorter hours and only twenty-one for the thirty shillings a week. When the voting results were announced to the membership, a "loud and prolonged cheering" broke forth. We have caught up with the later stage of the Ten Hour Movement. The workers want more time off even at the expense of more money.

What was in the back of their mind was recapturing a bit of their old independence. The rapidly growing towns were as yet no more than overgrown villages. In them the worker kept his country mentality. He earned with the intention to spend on the subsistence level and to play as though his town were the old village. Only by a stretch of the modern meaning would we call him a worker. Driven from house and land, faced with starvation, he moved from his village to the nearest larger one; his children went from there to a town; their more numerous children from town to an industrial center. He, the original villager, never became a real factory worker. His armor was impermeable. He never succumbed. In his children, though, he had an Achilles' heel. Had it not been for child labor the eighteenth-century industrialists would not have taken the strides they did.

In an agricultural economy children had always been workers. For them were reserved the light tasks—chasing the crows, feeding the pigs, bringing home the cows. In trade and handicrafts too they were employed, and at long hours, but with all the slowness and irregularity of preindustrial working habits. In fact, income then was not individual but family income. The family was considered at work all together, and their earnings made an indivisible pool. In a domestic industry like weaving everybody in the family worked. Whenever they thought of their income, it was as a unit, so that if they made more than enough all together, they never thought of removing children or wives from the work and letting the man carry it alone. Rather would they all take shorter hours together. With the appearance of the oversized workshops that served as the first factories, it was not at all contrary to family morality to put children to work too. The capitalist did not tear children from their mother's laps; mothers sent their children to him. For a time, specially wherever the whole family worked in the same place, abuses did not appear. With the splitting up of the family, control went from the parents to the owners.

Parents should have known better, perhaps, than to separate themselves from the children. They did it not so much because they were starving, or because their senses were blunted by the miserable life they led—though both these possibilities held true to some extent. It was also that, coming from the village as they did, the possibility of exploitation of children by grown men was not immediately suspected. However, it soon became clear that no compassion like that of parents for children ruled the heart of the factory owner. Whereas the adult could not be broken to factory work easily, the child's habits had not yet been firmly formed. He could be trained—by force if necessary—to heed the machine. After a time children became more valuable than adults. The first advantage was their cheapness, the second their adaptability to factory discipline. So they went from cotton mills to mines to potteries to the matchmaker's. Eventually Parliament rescued them. Eventually, but by then industry had found its labor force, and the next generation had been trained in proper work habits.

The Ten Hour Movement did do one thing. It crystallized the workday and in so doing crystallized free time too. At the time it was stirring up textile workers, the less developed industries worked longer hours, some of them, but in the old style. The working day, a jellylike substance, could hardly be called a notion, much less a concept. Without much machinery, the workshops then would seem to a present-day observer like a hangout for pieceworkers. A carpet factory or a pinworks took off a half-day on Saturday. A tobacco works had no hours except those the workers made. A pipe factory would be open from six in the morning to eight in the evening; the workers came and left when they pleased; the place was usually empty at 7:00 P.M. What time the workers had in which to do nothing must have been like the spare time of nonindustrial days. When work is not fixed by machines, unoccupied time appears every now and then, somewhat as a surprise, but as a surprise one expects occasionally without knowing just when it will come.

The idea of a pastime fits spare time well—some little thing to do when what you had to do didn't take as long as you thought. To pass spare time people also knew of longer-range things to do that could be picked up and dropped at will— knitting an undershirt, for example. Many a housewife, having finished her tasks earlier than expected—perhaps because a rain prevented her from hanging the wash—used to sit down to knit, and, given like good fortune for a neighbor, to chat. Our shoemaker had shoes to make or repair. When he was playing cards at the alehouse he wasn't making shoes, but neither was he spending free time. Time in the modern sense had no part of the scheme. He had shoes to make, ale to drink, and cards to play, all of which he did without need of the words work and leisure. What the ten-hour workman now had, though, was free time, a lump of concentrated nothingness he never had before. Work time and free time are now split, to remain so till this day.

All during the sixteenth to eighteenth centuries, riots to restore the commons took place in England. The spirit of enclosure, however, was rampant. In 1786 an observer predicted that in half a century more an open field or undivided common would be a rarity. The countryman-worker in his quest for free time wanted to retain some of his old life. At first, his nostalgia could be relieved, at least in part. In the old villages there had been cockfighting, badger baiting, whippet racing, coursing, hunting, fishing, and bowling, fighting matches, football, quoits, and dancing in the streets. The worker's hopes for a return to these pleasures were soon dimmed. His troubles had begun when he lost his space, the ground he thought he and his family had a right to, his native ground, his place in the world. He got back neither that space nor a new one to measure up to it.[3]

As the town grew and spread out, the worker kept losing space. Though he never fully realized it, by losing space he lost money and time. The open spaces in the towns were soon replaced by enclosures. After the sons of sons of the villagers piled into the big towns, after numerous, dispersed workshops came to be concentrated into a few central factories, there was little left but dirty streets. Unlike France and Italy, with whom ancient Rome left an urban tradition, and where, in some of their cities, one still drinks the same clear water piped in by Roman engineers, England knew nothing of city management. With squalor all about, said a student of this period, it was no wonder that, when they woke up to the fact, the English thought "soap was civilization."[4] In the era before railroads the densest population in the cities huddled around rivers, canals, or ports, and in its middle rose the center of industry. By the 1850s, with hordes encamped in wooden shacks on either side of former cart tracks, where was the worker to enjoy the free time he had won from the Ten Hour Act? The boating of those who lived on Thamesside was cut down by river traffic. Bowling on the roads

3. Hannah Arendt in *Human Condition* (Chicago: University of Chicago Press, 1958), discusses the history of the idea of property here described as held by the villager. The riots over the loss of commons are documented by Eggleston, *Transit of Civilization*.

4. The remark about the English linking of soap and civilization is Chapman's.

stepped aside for wheeled traffic. Gambling was almost unknown, testified London's Commissioner of Police. As to
gambling houses, "I know of none," he said, tongue-in-cheek,
"except the Stock Exchange may be so considered."

All the things the villager used to do for sports and recreation required space. A millwright who had once been on the
Continent complained that there was nothing in Manchester
a man could do on Sunday but go to the public house, and go
with the intention of getting drunk, sitting and drinking glass
after glass; in France and Switzerland, where he had worked,
people went to dances and had games and different recreations at the places they went to, and cheerfully enjoyed
themselves, he said, drinking but little. There were no games
in Manchester, and no open spaces.[5]

By this time Sunday had become the deadest day of the
week. "Sunday is our great difficulty," said one witness testi-
fying on public houses, "we cannot get over Sunday." The
Reformation had seen to making the day a dismal bore, and
enterprising businessmen thought that the move was in the
right direction. One of the first steps in the right direction
was Luther's assertion that the only holiday to be observed
was Sunday. The medieval calendar would never have suited
a business calendar—there were too many holidays. Lowering the saints down to mortality was another step in the
direction of improving the calendar. If Christian martyrs
never made sainthood, their day was no different from any-
one else's. But back to Sunday. In 1856 Sunday band concerts
began in the London parks. The Archbishop of Canterbury
objected and they were stopped. (At that time the resident
of many a small town in Sicily could hear over 100 band
concerts a year in the main square.) In the same year the
Commons rejected overwhelmingly a proposal to open the

5. The quotations of the Commissioner of Police and the traveling millwright appear also in Chapman's *Culture and Survival*.

British Museum and the National Gallery after Sunday morning services. This was a day to be spent in silence and meditation, not in having mass first and then enjoying oneself by singing, dancing, talking, drinking, or doing whatever the day offered. The word *holiday* in its origin implies dancing.[6]

With all the joy gone out of the Lord's day, it might as well not have existed. To take all joy out, one must say, seems too often to have been precisely the purpose. The thought seems to have been that if there were nothing but work for a man to do, he would no longer see any point to stopping work once he had earned the exact number of pennies he needed. In fact in some areas Sunday did not exist. According to Andrew Carnegie, by 1866 every ton of pig iron made in the world, except in two establishments, was made by men working in double shifts of twelve hours each, having neither Sunday nor holiday the year round. Thus one of the earliest shorter-workweek laws on record was violated, that of Moses. The strategy of the gloomy holiday in many cases did succeed in being perpetuated for over a century. Many more workers turned to drink. Slow suicide seemed to be the answer.[7]

Fortunately there were those who were not so blind as to miss the chance of profit. The period roughly from 1850 to 1900 reveals a *volte-face* by an increasing number of businessmen and investors. The original idea of the early manufacturers and bankers had been that the best way to get a good day's work out of hands was to encourage thriftiness, abstemiousness, and seriousness. A new group appeared on

6. The gloomy holiday strategy reappears on this side of the ocean in legislation the remnants of which still exist in various parts of the country as "Blue Laws." See Carl N. Degler, *Out of Our Past* (New York: Harper & Row, 1959). For the religious and cosmological significance of the holiday see Pieper, *Leisure;* and Roger Caillois, *L'homme et le sacré: "La fête est la chaos retrouvé et façonné a nouveau."*

7. On drink and alcoholism in Europe, see Henry Carter, *Europe's Revolt against Alcohol* (London: Kelly, 1915), and Hermann Levy, *Drink: An Economic and Social Study* (London: Routledge, 1951).

the scene now, whose pockets would fill more quickly if the
worker, once the day's work was done, became a spender, an
imbiber, and frivolous. A state of affairs that enabled this
group to earn honest money deserved a better name than
idleness. From this time on, with opportunity knocking, the
word idleness crawls out of its ugly cocoon to turn into a
beautiful butterfly—leisure.

The possibilities in commercial sports were not perceived
immediately. What first attracted attention may have been
the crowds of thousands that flocked to amateur games,
whereas only hundreds had come before. Those games, like
horse racing, essentially spectator sports to begin with, attracted villagers to the commons in crowd proportions. The
profit in refreshment stands may have touched off the
thought—in someone with money—of hiring or, better, buying tracks, and so on. Persons began to organize games that
had existed as country or aristocratic sports. Football, once
the game of former public-school boys, horse racing, the
sport of princes, boxing—recall that the rules were established by the Marquis of Queensberry—golf, a game played
by Scottish kings—these all became, as the saying goes,
moneymaking propositions. And to them the workers
turned, abandoning their quoits, bowls, and rabbit coursing
and the host of other games they had played for nothing or
for the beer with their skittles. They had to go farther and
farther away to enjoy them too. Most of the small racetracks
had gone under. The big ones took their stand where the
railroad could bring out the crowds. The worker was now
making more money and had his free time in one chunk each
day. His own space was gone; even the space he could afford
to rent to stand or sit on for a few hours was taking him a long
time to get to. He was beginning to lose time and money
along with his space.

With the new diversions came new publications, magazines and dailies like *Sporting Life* and the *Sportsman*. Nei-

ther producing nor paying for things like games and magazines fell within the old notions of production as something having to do with agriculture or industry. If these last two categories be considered as phases in an economic evolution, then the third phase, devoted to giving such services as sports and sports magazines, sometimes called the tertiary stage by economists, came to prominence in the twentieth century in the production and purchasing of travel, recreation, art, literature, science, philosophy, personal, and government services.[8]

Before we get ahead of ourselves, we had better recall that the worker, deprived of his customary space, yearned for the pleasures he used to get from it. He was willing to spend part of his good money for them too—both by taking time off from work and by paying for his sports on the barrelhead. But, rural man that he was, he was not ready to let loose of his purse strings. Yet by the end of the nineteenth century he began buying more food and drink and clothes. Not only did his intake of food increase, but he got his calories through more exotic and costly imports like bananas, oranges and lemons, cocoa, and others. Variety, too, appears in all categories. More than one kind of dog biscuit turns up on the market, thus making possible the rarefied choice of dog biscuits. The number of persons employed in the preparation and distribution of foodstuffs went up far beyond anything ever seen before. At the same time all sorts of inventions and schemes for goods or services began to be patented or to seek investment, from the preserving of lobster to the hiring out

8. For the "tertiary stage" concept in economics, see Allan G. B. Fisher, *Economic Progress and Social Security* (London: Macmillan, 1945); for a more recent concept of stages in which "the age of high mass consumption" appears as the parallel, see W.W. Rostow, *The Stages of Economic Growth* (London: Cambridge University Press, 1960). For criticism of current trends in the manufacturing of goods and wants in the United States, see John K. Galbraith, *The Affluent Society* (Boston: Houghton Mifflin, 1958).

of toboggans or the promoting of musical comedies. Many
had their start as limited liability companies, only to fall by
the wayside, but others survived and when they did, pros-
pered so as to encourage newcomers to ignore the cadavers
strewn about. Something must have happened to break the
habit of oatmeal, herring, and potatoes. Changes were going
on indeed.

The improvement in roads and rails made it practical for
a businessman to extend the range of his products. More
important were causes stemming from urban concentration.
One would guess that the purse of the second-generation city
dweller had little more chance of being parted from its
owner than it had from the owner's father. It was not enough,
though it did help, to be able to flash new things before his
eyes. But if to get a house to live in he had to commit himself
to a high rent, there was not much to do except open the
purse.

The squalor of the city camps led to plague and disease.
The municipalities finally had to provide sewerage, lighting,
and pavement. Newly arrived hordes of immigrants stayed
in the outskirts. They had to find ways to get to the factory.
The problem of the time and expense of the journey to work
wheeled into sight. The bicycle appeared not long before this
time. Originally an article of luxury, like the automobile
later, it soon became a necessity for workers. Housing also
began to make further incursions on the budget. Cottages
were torn down to make way for factory and office buildings.
Tenements were built. They seemed to have advantages
over the cottages—running water perhaps—but required a
higher rent.

The use of the word *tenement* for the new big housing
buildings is ironically appropriate. The word comes from Old
French, meaning a holding or a fief. Its special connection
with land emphasizes that the new space allotted for a rent
to the second-generation townsman was nothing like the old

holding. The cost and rent of land in the industrial centers kept going up with the entrance of each immigrant. Stories began to be piled one on the other. A "flat" meant a story. Then flats began to get smaller so that there could be more than one on a single flat. *Apartment* was a word signifying an even smaller piece. The process whereby the ceiling descended and the walls closed in was beginning. Today we would think that compared to ours the space in those flats, apartments, and rooms was enormous.

It was no use crying for the cheaper and roomier living of the cottages. The cottages weren't there any more. So the workingman had to open his purse wider for diversion, rent, health, and a bicycle. Businessmen began to discover that with a higher cost of living the workman sticks to his loom. His family as a result was seemingly better housed, for instance. The secret of this improvement of the worker's lot, though, was that he could not choose to be housed as he was before, neither better nor worse. The kind of shelter he once had no longer existed. Nor, given the lack of a city tradition in England, were large squares set up where people could gather to talk and children could run around in play. The hardness of England's lack of sunshine probably helped remove this solution from the mind, but, sun or no sun, squares could have been used by adults at least half the year and by children all year round.[9]

Not only were goods and men moving faster and farther because of improved communications, but machinery was moving faster too. The standardization of screws and parts speeded the mechanization of industry. It also made the machinery run faster. All industries turned to machinery.

9. London did get some fine examples of squares and crescents from Christopher Wren and after him from James and Robert Adam. The advocacy of squares and piazzas is sustained by Camillo Sitte in *Der Städe-Bau* (Vienna, 1899); in the English version C. T. Stewart, trans., *The Art of Building Cities* (New York: Reinhold, 1945).

The old-fashioned workshops died on their feet. The new products like the bicycle which came to life in the hands of artisans passed quickly into the maw of machinery. Thus more and more workers were pulled in and introduced to the regular discipline of factory life. Work everywhere became more intense, free time more completely cut off from work and space, and it, too, more intense.

The villager had no problem of free time. He knew what to do with whatever amount he had. But no one, least of all himself, quite knew what to do with the worker's free time, primarily because no one grasped what he had become. That he was until recently a rustic, everyone knew. The first attempts to get his money used the games of the past on a larger, commercial scale. But they were not enough. He was less of a player in these new sports. Moreover he himself had changed. The new work had made him a man of different habits and necessities. It had reduced the worker's habitat and that, too, brought changes in him. The significance of some of these changes was better seen at that time than it is now. At least the problems were discussed in public. There were other important changes. In 1870 the Education Act insured the worker against illiteracy. From then on learning how to read and write was part of the program for everybody. The program itself was what was known as democracy. It had suffered a slight setback in England nearly a hundred years before because of the excesses, real and imagined, of the French Revolution. The aristocratic fear of the Jacobins could not hold out long against the commercial cry for equality. The opportunity to learn to read was one of the first equalities sought, and though the opportunity later could be better described as compulsory, everyone learned to read, at least to read a newspaper. As it happened, this was enough, and also important. Its results were less clearly foreseen. The man had money in his pocket. He was learning to spend it for things like bicycles, football games, and rent. Besides the bread and meat to keep his family going, what else would he buy? This was a difficult question and remains so today.

Perplexity of this kind troubled the men who were out to make money with the money or credit they already had at the bank. They had seen the success of some shots in the dark, but they had seen more fiascos. Obviously this kind of market was capricious. It was different from cloth or shoes. As population had grown thicker, businessmen had experimented tentatively with advertising by handbilling or posting simple notifications of the existence of certain goods and services. Their efforts fit the etymology of the word *advertising:* to draw attention to or inform. Once the tax on advertising in newspapers was lifted in the 1850s, there were some efforts in that medium as well, for things like insurance, watches, wines, and spirits, commodities then of interest to persons of more wealth than workers. In fact the newspaper reader at that time was of the educated classes. As reading spread and the halfpenny paper arrived, advertising perked up. By the turn of the century its era had begun. It had already begun in America.

In the United States no "taxes on knowledge" like the advertising or stamp taxes held back the progress of industry. The British got rid of them only in 1861. England can lay claim to have taken the first steps in modern advertising, but America soon afterward set the pace. As early as the first decade of the 1900s American newspapers loaded half their space with advertising. The English today are still shocked to see a whole-page newspaper ad.

Machinery, too, in America took a more audacious stride. There was more free land to be had in America than in England, to be sure, and this indeed held back the progress of labor unions. Given the availability of land and the shortage of labor, the first known strike in America, at Philadelphia in the building trades, was set off by a demand for a

shorter day's work—from six in the morning to six at night
—plus (and here we come again to a familiar pattern) a demand for extra pay for overtime. So as early as 1791 the
question of shorter hours appears. A quarter of a century
later the journeymen millwright and machine workers of
Philadelphia met at a tavern and passed a resolution that ten
hours of labor were enough for one day. Their ten hours
though, went again from 6 A.M. to 6 P.M., allowing "an hour
for breakfast and one for dinner." In Philadelphia, New York,
Boston, and elsewhere such strikes and protests went on
sporadically, and before the middle of the nineteenth century one could speak of a ten-hour movement in the eastern
United States.[10]

As long as the open West existed, little could be done on
a national scale. It was not until the end of the century that
the ten-hour day established itself in a majority of industries.
Many pockets of resistance held out in industries like steel,
cotton, baking, lumber, and the railroads. With land to the
west and a labor shortage, manufacturers were ever on the
lookout for laborsaving machinery. Given a vast population
without a parish system to sustain it, an uprooted population
that had gone from emigration to the United States into
migration within it, the adaption of men to machines went
somewhat easier than in England. To men, time, and machines nearly a whole chapter will be devoted later on. It is
advertising on which we now should turn our gaze.

Advertising in its original sense does this: it informs that
goods are accessible. It is a stentorian peddler whose voice
must ring not across mere village lanes at 8:30 in the morning

10. On the history of the movements for ten-hour and eight-hour workdays in the United States, see John R. Commons and Associates, *History of
Labour in the United States,* 4 vols. (New York: Macmillan, 1918–1935); S.
Perlman, "Shorter Hours Movement," *Encyclopedia of the Social Sciences;*
and U.S. Congress, Senate, Subcommittee of the Committee on the Judici-
ary, *The Thirty-Hour Workweek,* January 1933.

but day and night over the din of the city and the breadth of the land. One manufacturer with machinery could now supply a whole nation with his products. He would be rich if they but knew of his wares (an easy task given literacy and the cheap newspaper), and wanted them (not nearly so easy). Advertising became a success. It made people buy at a rate that more than paid for the advertising, and this was what counted for the businessman.[11]

To make people buy it is not enough to put goods in front of them. How to account for advertising success, then? We have seen that farmers and villagers were ejected from their land and hearth, and sought sustenance in growing industrial centers. Their work grew concentrated, their free time blocked off and set in a constricted space. The first wedge into their purse, fattened on the job, was driven by commercial diversions and an ineluctable higher standard of living. They would buy diversions, then, but which diversions? With bread and coal one knew how much people had bought last year and had a fair idea of how much they would eat this year or heat the house next winter, but how many if any, would buy an article just invented called roller skates? Though the market for diversions had tempting possibilities, it was too risky. If only a way could be found to make it less capricious. Advertising was the answer. It had merely to wave the di-

11. For the history of advertising in the United States as well as England, see Henry Sampson, *A History of Advertising from the Earliest Times* (London: Chatto and Windus, 1874); Frank S. Presbey, *The History and Development of Advertising* (Garden City, N.Y.: Doubleday, 1929); E. S. Turner, *The Shocking History of Advertising!* (New York: Dutton, 1953); and Edgar R. Jones, *Those Were the Good Old Days* (New York: Simon and Schuster, 1959). For more recent decades in the United States, see Martin Mayer, *Madison Avenue, U.S.A.* (New York: Harper, 1958); Editors of Fortune, *The Amazing Advertising Business* (New York: Simon and Schuster, 1957); Herbert Marshall McLuhan, *The Mechanical Bride* (New York: Vanguard, 1951); and Otto Klepper, *Advertising Procedure* (Englewood Cliffs, N.J.: Prentice-Hall, 1952).

verting quality of its wares in front of readers to find buyers galore.

Here advertising goes beyond saying merely that a certain good exists and can be had; it also points out what the good is good for—as the free-time possibilities of a new car, a perfume, a book, a radio, a horse race, a cigar, and even lectures. A peddler would do this in trying to seduce an onlooker into buying from his cart.

Advertising had another appeal to make, it was soon learned. In the new world of cities there was danger of being lost as a person, as someone whom others knew something about and respected. Whatever shortcomings the villager suffered from, anonymity was not one of them. Aristocracy, where one's status is fairly well known at a glance, had no such trouble either. These were worlds of position. In them one *is* somebody. What one is, or stands for, can be told not solely by house, field, shop, or clothes but also by language, manners, and antecedents. Finding themselves in the city, farmers and villagers had no field or shop, nor clothes or antecedents that made sense to neighbors themselves uprooted and from strange regions. Not even their games were the same. It is like having a group of people together who after a few drinks feel like singing but don't know the same songs—one or two start singing a tune; the others don't know it and remain silent and frustrated until the song peters out. Another few begin a new song. It meets the same fate. After a while everyone gives up. The advertiser is he who in such circumstances says, "Look here, I have a printed songbook with new songs; it costs only a dime, and, think of it, now you can all sing together." If for the last line he substitutes a picture of rich people singing from the new songbook —or drinking a whisky, or standing alongside a car—he is changing his tactic to one of snobbery. This last aspect of advertising could and did become important only because of the anonymity of the city, where no one knew another and also, and more fundamental, because antecedents and land, the marks of the aristocracy, had given way to new insignia —production and money. In a society where equality of birth was the order of the day, where long-established patterns of meeting and dealing with people were gone, money became the coin of status.[12]

Money can be spent on many things—a fur coat, flowers, a mistress, a do-it-yourself kit, an automobile. Which of these reflect prestige, which are the mark of the worthies? Equality of birth had nothing to do with remaining equal. The prizes in life went to those who succeeded in moving upward on a ladder runged with money and prestige. Those who won success were supposed also to have won happiness and perhaps even the favor of God. With mobility rather than station the secret of life's treasures, movement pressed upward. If it could not go upward much or at all, or went down, at least by working hard and skimping on some things one could *pretend* a distinction to oneself and to others by purchasing some of the signs of success. Not many had contact with the elect. The contact in itself was a sign. The advertisers seemed to have many contacts among the worthies. Products began

12. "Status panic" is what Mills calls the exceptional need for status in the white collar class. In discussing the attitudes of professional classes toward consumption, a distinction must be made between the old and the new (the bureaucratized) professional class. See Emil Lederer and Jacob Marschak, *The New Middle Class* ("Der Neue Mittelstand," *Grundriss der Sozialökonomik*, 9 Abteilung 1, 1926), trans. S. Ellison (New York: Columbia University WPA Project, 1937); Hans Speier, "The Salaried Employee in Modern Society," *Social Research* (February 1934); Roy Lewis and Angus Maude, *The English Middle Classes* (New York: Knopf, 1950); Carl Dreyfuss, *Salaried Employee;* T. H. Marshall. "The Recent History of Professionalism in Relation to Social Structure and Social Policy," *Canadian Journal of Economics and Political Science,* reprinted in *Readings in American Social Classes,* ed. Robert C. Angell (Ann Arbor, Mich.: University of Michigan Press, 1945); A. M. Carr-Saunders and P. A. Wilson, *The Professions* (Oxford: Clarendon Press, 1933); and Harold D. Lasswell, "The Moral Vocation of the Middle-Income Skill Group," *Ethics* (January 1935).

to be placed in a snobbish setting; the purchaser felt the comfort of believing that their exhibition (a fur coat or costly carpet) or use (a high-rent house, a witticism from a fashionable comedy) put one closer to those one needed to associate with in order to be judged successful.[13]

A third pertinent need that advertising exploited was the saving of time. Proponents of industry had tried to soften the impact of machinery on men by praising its laborsaving assets. Machinery that saves men's labor, they also argued, usually saves their time. We have seen that one of the oldest fears of workers is that the machine may save too much time and thus throw nearly everyone into unemployment. The wave of enthusiasm for individual devices evidently brought no such danger and if they appeared to save both labor and

13. The subject of workingmen's consumption has a long history in sociology and economics beginning with Quetelet and LePlay's studies, moving through Engels's formation of the ratio of luxuries and necessities into "Engels's Law," to Keynes's concern with the business cycle. A brief history of consumer expenditures can be found in W. S. Woytinsky and E. S. Woytinsky, *World Population and Production* (New York: Twentieth Century Fund, 1953). The workingman's attitude toward consumption can be studied from statistical breakdowns in the Wharton or *Life* expenditure surveys. In addition to studies already cited such as Richard Hoggart, *Uses of Literacy* (Harmondsworth, Eng.: Penguin, 1958); Lee Rainwater et al., *Workingman's Wife* (Oceana, N.Y., 1959); William F. Whyte et al., *Men, Money, and Motivation* (New York: Harper & Row, 1955); Zweig, *British Worker;* Chinoy, *Automobile Workers;* and Berger, *Working-Class Suburb;* see Carl C. Zimmerman, *Consumption and Standard of Living* (New York: Van Nostrand, 1936); R. Centers and Hadley Cantril, "Income and Income Aspiration," *Journal of Abnormal and Social Psychology* 41 (1946); Hazel Kyrl, *A Theory of Consumption,* (Boston: Houghton Mifflin, 1923); Herman P. Miller, *Income of the American People* (New York: Wiley, 1955); David Riesman and Howard Roseborough, "Careers and Consumer Behavior," in *Consumer Behavior,* eds. Lincoln H. Clark and Nelson N. Foote (New York: New York University Press, 1954–1961); George Katona, *Psychological Analysis of Economic Behavior* (New York: McGraw-Hill, 1951); Pierre Martineau, "Social Classes and Spending Behavior," *Journal of Marketing* 23, 2 (1958); and Joint Committee on the Economic Report, *Characteristics of the Low Income Population and Related Federal Programs.*

time they rode in on the great wave of mechanical enthusiasm. The automobile obviously saved time because it got you to work and back home and to and from shopping faster. Household appliances also comprised a notable group. The refrigerator saved daily traffic with the iceman as well as daily shopping at the stores; the carpet sweeper saved the time and muscle used in beating the rug; automatic furnaces spared the back and the time spent in stoking; hot running water saved time lost by heating it in a kettle. Timesaving was a successful pitch because it had the prestige of industry and science, and, not to be forgotten, because the worker in his mobile state had always less time than his official job time made believe.

The appeals of advertising are limited only by man's ingenuity and conscience. No advertiser openly recommended spending money on a mistress one can boast about. Not that mistresses in any age have the reputation of being stingy with their protector's money. Indeed they rival the modern consumer. Though at first a related kind of personal advertisement did prosper, advertisers could not encourage this kind of conduct among those who bought a halfpenny paper. It would be immoral, and besides, the whole system would topple. The most the advertiser will do in these days is to suggest buying things for a lovely female whose relation to the male is left vague. The hawker at a fair, now, he will gladly propose such a purpose for his brilliants to a man who looks like the right type. The hawker can make his pitch to the individual, the advertiser cannot, but both carry big bags of tricks. My selecting three of their appeals here was to show how advertising succeeded in getting people to buy many things in a way their forefathers would have condemned as damned foolishness.

In advertising, the producer of goods and services had an instrument that helped him take some of the freakishness out of the market. For a time the advertiser had chiefly the newspaper to puff his wares. Then along with improvements in printing came the radio and after that television. As for television, the advertisers themselves pushed and subsidized its invention; they helped bring it into the world, having seen in radio a preview of home-penetrating power. The film, too, has been their ally in a telling manner. Almost without exception the makers of feature films have not been subsidized by advertisers, yet so urgent has the need been to prove one's success in life through the buying of goods that filmmakers have unwittingly catered to the public. They have put heroes and heroines in so costly a context that at times it would be impossible to find any person or group living at that level of expenditures . . . except in the movies. Since these films are exported, great masses of nonindustrialized peoples have got the impression that all of northern Europe and North America lives in that high style. We ourselves have had it so much with us from the childhood of our cinema days that it escapes us completely.

All of which conveys that people would stop, look, and listen at advertisements even if, as with the films, there were nothing to sell. In fact much effort and money today goes into so-called institutional or good-will advertising. A steel or chemical company may advertise not to sell its wares—of which they sell enough—but to build up the corporate image, as they say, to keep the public (for the moment not a consumer) from forgetting the service the company performs to the nation or to national defense or to humanity, science, and progress. And sometimes a company advertises on this scale because the owner or his wife wants the personal satisfaction of being nationally recognized or simply thought more of by their friends at the country club. All these efforts go into the dollar totals for advertising, but a better name for them is publicity.

Another twentieth-century ally of the advertiser has been the installment plan. Through it or other schemes of deferred payment, the worker commits his future money and time. Title to the goods may come in the future too, but he feels, and, more important, looks to others, as if he were the owner in the present. In any case, wear and tear begins with his signature.

Of the 100 or more most important inventions exploited commercially in the twentieth century, about one-third were laborsaving and about one-half were in the field of consumer goods—the phonograph, rayon, nylon, the radio, and television. At the same time the occupations that have seen the greatest increase in personnel have been the so-called service industries. This reflects not only a greater demand for games, toys, entertainments, sports, motors, cameras, and government social services, but also the rising importance of an in-between class of persons who live on salaries, keep their hands free of grease and grit, and experience less of the work pacing that mechanized jobs impose on workers. This category, not too precise in its limits, has been variously called the *petit bourgeoisie*, the *salariat*, the lower middle class, or the white-collar worker. When we have talked about workers in general, we have usually included this group of them that came to prominence in the 1900s.

Because of their position as straddlers between upper and lower classes they feel it necessary to distinguish themselves by all moral and legitimate means from the workers. Unlike the proletariat, but like the aristocracy, the *salariat* has a fixed income; like the proletariat's and unlike the aristocracy's it comes from a boss, however impersonal. The aristocrat's income came from the rent rolls. In money the salaried sometimes earn more, sometimes less, than the wage earner. Their means of distinction lies in their cleaner hands, the relation of their job to literacy and the ancient scribe, their different work clothes, and a careful selection of the insignia money can buy—education, flowers, house, furnishings, and neighborhood—and to be able to point out to a stranger that the man he is looking at or talking to works but is not a worker.

Paradoxically the ethic of work made more progress with this group, concerned as it was to adopt the opinions of those who stood at the top of the new hierarchy—the producers and the moneyed. Vulnerability to the snobbery in advertising is greatest in this class of persons. Their conduct has given rise to the concept of the nation as a group of consumers. The concept exaggerates in implying that everyone acts as a member of the class.

Everyone may be a consumer, but those who consume most consumer goods are the salaried, not the wage earners or the professional classes, although these others have also been led down the spending path by one or more vulnerabilities to advertising. The working class in England still clings to the doctrine of enough money to live on and a little for the frills; the professional classes still hold to values they put above buying things with money. The class we have been describing, too, does not consider money its highest aim, otherwise at times it would turn to the higher pay of the worker. What it needs is a clarification of position, and its chief method is to buy and exhibit the goods and services proclaimed by advertising to be those of the on-high.

Wherever one talks of category or class, large or small, one is bound to ignore the exceptions and make everything sound too simple. That a physician can cater to rich widows, or a worker indulge in silk pajamas and Havana cigars, or a foreman or office manager give in to oatmeal, may not be novel, but is still exceptional. By their earning power many classes of workers soon left behind their brethren who remained in comparative poverty. The affluent worker's resistance to spending crumbles at the advertiser's approach, but less easily to the snobbery appeal than to the other two we have identified—recreation and timesaving.

More or less the same kinds of goods are advertised today

as were at the birth of the halfpenny newspaper. In the United States, the most heavily advertised products—each representing at least $10 million a year of advertising billing —are soap, drugs and cosmetics, foods, soft drinks, automobiles, home appliances, alcoholic beverages, and tobacco. In England at the century's turn the *Evening News* and *Daily Mail* advertised Vinolia soap, Bovril, Vi cocoa, bicycles, tricycles, and sewing machines on installment-plan terms. (In 1892, the *Evening News* added a new service for the readers —a Saturday football supplement.)

From the very beginning in the United States, solid manufacturers and bankers were suspicious of advertising. Today, in durable goods, where men from production, engineering, and finance rule the roost, the advertiser is looked on with disdain. In soaps and cigarettes he is treated with respect. Consumer goods still describes the area where advertising makes its heaviest sales contribution.

As there is a continuity in kind of goods sold, so is there in tactics. We still see advertising using the same three charms it acquired soon after birth in the industrial era. Things to buy to use in free time (current examples: awnings on the patio, gracious living, travel in the style of the new active leisure, the thrill of an outboard motor), things that mark the buyer as a person to be looked up to (brand of soap, cigarettes, consumers' guides, books, perfume, house furnishings, cars), and things that save time (the automatic dishwasher, the electric saw, the deep freezer). These appeals have variations. For instance, a patent medicine offers to pep people up, stirring them to buy through the fear that tiredness is abnormal and makes one a failure at the energetic work and play so much a part of success. All in all they have done much of the job of turning the American into a spender. If you ask the American why he works when he could have time off, the answer is that there is something or other he needs. At one time he may have needed extra work to pay the medical bills for an accident or to set something aside for a rainy day or for his children's schooling. This argument has been weakened by unemployment compensation, pensions, social security, public schooling, insurance of all kinds borne and advocated by government, industry, the church, and the family. While not eliminating the need for emergency money, these provisions have had a reassuring effect on fears of emergencies. The part they have played in opening up the American's wallet has not been well recognized. They too, along with the cinema and the installment plan, have been allies of the advertiser. Without rainy days ahead, the old kind when it could pour for years at a time, the American need not fear opening his wallet wider. No, money for medical bills or even a nest egg is not likely to be his answer. He works because there's something he needs, or, he might simply say, because he needs money. And what does he need money for? To buy things, of course.

Certainly there are activities that don't require money. Mushroom collecting, for instance, a favorite sport of the Russians. Loafing is another inexpensive activity. The advertisers don't recommend it except as the reward for buying a plane ticket to some place where people are said to sleep under sombreros all the while the sun's up, the kind of place that for some reason is thought to be particularly restful or at least picturesque to American tourists. In the United States, where loafing would cost nothing, it is not considered good form. Time is money, if for no other reason than that if you loaf you don't earn money.

Can't the American buy free time with the money he earns? By working shorter hours and taking less pay, it would be as though he paid a substitute to go to work for him part-time. The American doesn't need all the money he makes just to live, does he? We are back to the question with which the last chapter closed. In the U.S.S.R. to earn a loaf of bread the Russian must work much longer than the American for his loaf. Without quibbling over the relative nourishment in the two loaves, the difference should mean that the American can take his free time much sooner than the Russian, for he earns his daily bread in less time. Yet he does not take a workweek shorter than the Russian. Evidently the American has not bought much free time, or he buys only what he can get at a bargain rate, or solely when he can't get something else like employment security or higher wages in exchange. There's not likely to be the cheers the masons of Newcastle shouted out on hearing that their week was to be shorter, even though their pay envelope was to be lighter. If you loaf you can't buy things advertising dangles before your eyes, things you need to have, even if you must skimp on lunches to buy them.[14]

Of the three major reasons we have given for the success of advertising in helping turn the American into a consumer, the first and third—suggesting something to do in one's empty hours, and ways of saving other hours lost in the city's concentration of space and work—are clearly related to free time. The remaining reason, the appeal to snobbery, seems at first unrelated. Actually it is but one step removed. Its relation is to work. If one works, one has less time off work. Some union officials today say that one reason their men take on second jobs is that they have bought "major items" on the installment plan and are anxious to pay off. As a Spanish proverb puts it, *el hombre que trabaja pierde su tiempo*. The man who works loses his time. Consumption eats money, money costs work, work loses time. It's as simple as a nursery-rhyme chain of causes.

14. For the confusion caused at the inauguration of the seven-hour day in Moscow, see Osgood Caruthers, "Rubles and Free Time," *New York Times*, January 7, 1961. For some other aspects of "How Russians Relax," see Fred R. Bellmar, *Employee Recreation* 20, 7 (1959).

Leisure Activities and
Social Participation

ALAIN TOURAINE

Historians are usually content when they have traced the course of developments; when it comes to their implications and their meaning for our own society they tend to call upon a breed which is much more rare, and whose task is much more difficult —the social theorists. Among these the French sociologist Alain Touraine is one of the most widely respected. In the following selection we follow Touraine as he considers the contemporary significance of the emergence of leisure activities which have been emancipated from the constraints of traditional social life. Touraine looks at the intersection of leisure and some of the major phenomena which concern sociologists today: mass society, the character of work in an industrial order, social class,

SOURCE: Alain Touraine, *The Post-Industrial Society: Tomorrow's Social History: Classes, Conflicts, and Culture in the Programmed Society,* trans. Leonard F. X. Mayhew. (New York: Random House, Inc, 1971), pp. 193–208. Copyright © 1971 by Random House, Inc. Reprinted by permission of the publisher.

and the ethic of consumption. His work is indicative of the new attention which social scientists are giving to the question of leisure, and like all highly theoretical investigation points more to the asking of new questions than to the definitive settling of old ones.

If leisure activities are defined as activities other than work, one would have to include under the term most of the cultural acts of a society—religious life, games, political activity, and sports. Everyone rejects this definition without clearly defining why. The reasons will become clearer if we recall that the theme of leisure activity is almost always associated in the minds of sociologists with the subject of mass society. This is either because they are describing the subjection of individuals to the modern means of communication —mass media—or because they observe the effects of modern work, piecework, which is narrowly defined and performed within massive firms that are governed in such a way that the individual feels that he is connected with them only in terms of his function. These two themes are often connected with each other somewhat this way: the mechanization of work prepares the way for mechanized leisure, and leaves us helpless before the repeated onslaughts of propaganda (understood in the broadest sense).

Without discussing here the value or limitations of this analysis, we retain its general outlines: the question of leisure activities arises as soon as the members of a society come under cultural influences that are no longer connected with the organized activities of a concrete socioeconomic group. As a result, these cultural experiences are no longer understandable on the basis of the individual's professional and social experience.

One hesitates to compare the mass leisure activities of industrial and urban civilization with the folklore or cultural life or rural civilizations and nonindustrialized societies. In the latter, the content of the leisure activity is connected with professional and social life. Sometimes the activities are connected quite simply, as in seasonal holidays or celebrations connected with one's work; sometimes in an indirect manner, as when certain free-time activities are intended to compensate for unremitting labor or misery. This bond is almost always accompanied by another that unites free-time activities to the whole social life of the collectivity and usually has geographic reasons: a village feast reunites the inhabitants of a particular village, members of a concrete community. A festival in mining country may be an outlet for needs that are repressed by the work and the life in the mining villages; in any case it is profoundly integrated into the life of a working community.

This twofold rooting of leisure activities in lived social experience disappears in developed industrial civilizations, because of the development of communications techniques and because in cities or large urbanized zones, the individual is constantly thrown in, especially in his leisure activities, with people who do not belong to the same concrete professional or residential community. A great number of the cultural activities valued by our civilization no longer have their origin in professional activity but in the products of this activity. This change is connected with the most widespread aspect of professional evolution, the firm that produces for a vast market. The individual work is subordinated to the organization of production. Even if one can assure real participation by the workers in the decisions that direct the firm, the fact remains that professionally a very great number of workers or employees perform a task that gives them very little sense of participating in the creation of the finished product. The more techniques progress, the greater the distance between the individual working task and the product. In losing his professional autonomy, the worker has also lost one of the principles of his cultural autonomy. The work of the farmer, the miner, the carpenter gives these workers both satisfaction and dissatisfaction, burdens and sources of pride, that is, a properly professional experience that marks their lives, directly or indirectly, according to whether they are accepted or rejected. The regulated and compartmentalized work of the laborer or employee in the great mechanized organizations, on the other hand, no longer has any properly professional significance for the one who carries it out, and the worker reacts to his work in terms of the economic and social conditions under which he carries it out; in terms of the salary that he draws from it; the social relations, hierarchical or egalitarian, in which it places him; the rhythm in which he must perform it. Coal has no meaning except what the miner's work gives it; land is of no significance without the plow. But the importance of the automobile owes nothing to the work of the assembly-line workers and most often we do not know anything about the men, machines, and plants that produce the goods we seek to acquire and use in our leisure activities and in our entire life.

It may be tempting to oppose active leisure activities to passive leisure activities; these notions have at least the merit of isolating what is new in the present problem, the "passivity" of a great number of leisure activities. Following this line runs the risk of leading to generalizations that are loaded with presuppositions, if one does not at the outset define the meaning of this "passivity." The split between professional activities that have less and less independent meaning for a majority of workers and the cultural activities of the society in which they live must not be presumed but ascertained.

We are witnessing the weakening of cultural expressions bound to a particular social group. Nothing could be clearer than the decline of the traditional "worker-culture." Alert educators have replaced the idea of a worker-literature or a worker-culture with the much more realistic and fruitful description of workers participating in the total culture—which may mean participating in a movement of overall social and political opposition.

What is true on this level of "culture" is true on all the others. Whether it is material or nonmaterial culture, socioeconomic groups tend to define themselves more and more by their degree of participation in the activities and products of the culture, and less and less by possession of a subculture different from others. Social roles and cultural roles are more and more separate: categories like neighbor, skilled worker, native of a particular region, no longer explain the television viewer, the reader of the mass circulated paper, the automobile owner.

For the mass of semiskilled workers, participation in the culture is no longer based on professional life or traditional social role, but on consumption of items and products produced for the entire society. Efforts to redevelop the traditional roots only increases the distance between a man and the culture of the society, only increases his "passivity" in relation to mass leisure activities. Peculiarities are being washed aside and efforts to preserve or remake them are illusory. We must abandon this defensive attitude toward mass culture, for the belief that we can defend the autonomy of social groups against the new centers of cultural influence only supports the traditional class barriers.

Once past this temptation to nostalgia, how do we define leisure activities and how do we support any independence in the face of the increasing influence of the great public or private firms that determine the content and form of the cultural message? Is the greatest activity not also the most complete submission to styles of conduct increasingly engineered from the top of the society?

At first, the theme of cultural participation seems to answer this concern. Is not cultural underconsumption the lot of those on the bottom rungs of social stratification? How can one not admit, following Joffre Dumazedier,[1] the importance of simple physical recovery and of elementary social and familial obligations, material and other in a person's life outside of work? On returning from the plant or the office, one must rest, sleep, or relax, and one may have to clear the drain in the sink, stoke the furnace, or put the children to bed. Who could disagree that these obligations partially compensate for needs repressed by work and that they contribute to maintaining the physical and psychological balance of the individual? But the "active" creative value of these semileisure activities is limited, at least in the sense that they establish almost no bond between the one who performs them and the cultural values of his society.

Professional compensations—working in one's workshop and other hobbies—probably do not have the importance that some accord to them. On this, Georges Friedmann has made some subtle and disturbing remarks: one's work must possess some professional richness for the worker to seek compensation freely and actively in activities different from his job. Reduced models, like puttering in a workshop, are most often the activities of young men who anticipate that these activities will be of some value in the future. How many unskilled workers with no real trade, and no professional training in school or on the job, seek to create in their free time the substitutes for a professional life and trade that they do not possess? One can only respect them if it testifies to a desire for professional promotion. But is it correct to admire these activities if they mean nothing more than a backward look to a vanished past and if they are a substitute for more positive and active activities? A return to arts and crafts is as fallacious as the "Return to the Land" slogan of sad memory.

In a society of mass production and consumption, activity

1. Joffre Dumazedier, *Vers une civilisation du loisir* (Paris: Editions du Seuil, 1962).

or passivity depends less on which social group one belongs to and which cultural activities one indulges in than on the degree of social participation. One of the major points of interest in the study of leisure activity is to mark the limits and implications of the idea of social participation. The central idea of an analysis carried out in terms of either cultural participation or withdrawal is that today, when cultural values are attached to mass products, determined by a highly technical civilization with all its social problems, passivity is only the psychological expression of economic and social subjection or dependance.

Certain books and journals sometimes make it seem that only the workers and wage earners, of all those who are subjected to mass production, live amid a proliferation of leisure activities that numb, condition, and transform them. But we say the contrary and point out the extreme isolation of those with low incomes from the messages of the technical civilization. This is so because, since the production system is so complex and integrated, many workers on the jobs remain in their primary groups and, outside of work, television, newspapers, and magazines penetrate family life without modifying their relationship to the culture in any profound way. The multiplication of spectacles does not transform the spectator into an actor. The mass media do not try to modify attitudes and behavior. Anyway, surveys have shown that their effectiveness in this area is very limited when the ideas are not seconded by groups in which the subject is an active and involved member.

This social "passivity" is connected with the commercialization of leisure. In more general terms, it would be more accurate to say that the consumer on the whole has little control over the producer. The only weapon at his disposal is his refusal to consume; but this power is all the weaker as the consumer's attitude becomes more passive—in the case of the movies for example, when he sees more importance in going regularly than in the content of the film. This distance between the consumer and the producer, the consumer's frequent subjection to economic, moral, and political imperatives that are essentially conservative and mystifying, is the principal problem of a leisure civilization. But these reflections are not addressed to problems of the producer; they simply define the consumer's situation. From this point of view, one can suggest that the social groups that participate most weakly in sociocultural values are those most passively submissive to mass leisure activities as well as those most attached to family and neighbors, and to either the traditional or to a new type of cultural isolation. There is a connection between the two.

Exposure to mass leisure activities is greater among adolescents than among adults. This striking fact is inseparable from the major social phenomenon of the progressive appearance of adolescence as an autonomous social category in our society. If young workers and employees are not engaged in a really skilled trade, they no longer have to follow a social and professional apprenticeship. They immediately perform the work that they will carry out for the rest of their lives and often reach their top salary.

These young workers exhibit two principal characteristics: intense exposure to the mass media and the development of an extremely strong informal social organization. We can refer here to W. F. Whyte's beautiful book, *Street Corner Society*, a study of the social and cultural life of young men, sons of immigrants, especially Italians, living in a working-class section of Boston. Both the good and bad literature on teen-age gangs has shown to what degree the strengthening of primary social bonds—whether in accord with or in opposition to the law makes little difference—is connected with the weak degree of involvement of these adolescents in the society in which they live: as marginal individuals (for reasons having to do with their ethnic background and increas-

ingly also with their professional futures), they abandon all
effort to achieve broad socialization and content themselves
with a narrow socialization limited to the primary groups to
which they belong. This social and cultural retreat is too
often presented as "criminal"; it is much more often conservative. The evolution of premarital sexual relationships—dat-
ing in the United States, *pololeo* in Latin America—demon-
strates a tendency to the precocious stabilization of sexual
and emotional relations among adolescents; their behavior
approaches that of the adult: in the middle classes, the seven-
teen-year-old boy speaks of his girl and, partly thanks to
television, the couple is thus established—whatever may be
the degree of development in terms of the sexual relationship—recognized by parents, and accepted into the family.
Massive consumption of mechanized leisure activities, far
from causing a breakdown of primary social bonds, is actually
accompanied by a precocious development of such bonds.
Active participation in primary groups, of friends or neighbors, quasi-family, is only a compensation for weak social and
cultural activity. Exposure to mass leisure activities is the
expression both of this weak participation and of the desire
for greater participation in and contact with situations that
open up this closed world of gangs and families.

Membership in primary groups and highly structured
communities was the condition for creative participation in
social and cultural values in a society in which the culture was
a system of meanings directly attached to professional and
social experience; now, in a mass civilization, it is only the
expression of a forced cultural retreat and a weak participation in the general society.

One comes to the same realization if one considers more
broadly the differences in behavior among the social classes.
In a recent survey, I was struck with the slight importance
of leisure activity in the preoccupations of the workers: in the
responses, first, family life and, second, work occupied a

greater place. A study carried out in Kansas City and analyzed by Havighurst (in the *American Journal of Sociology* in 1957 and 1959) leads to the same conclusions. The workers appeared more "home-centered" and less "community-centered" than the middle class. The common image of American civilization fits with upper middle-class behavior; social stratification consequently marks differences in participation in community activities that are almost always led by such persons. These "home-centered" persons are not workers attached to a traditional culture based on profession; they are individuals who have neither the financial means nor the social motivations that move the middle class to the foreground of the social scene.

This American study suggests a comparison. In a society both open and conservative, cultural participation is bound to socioeconomic levels. But the mass media destroy this traditional bond. Those who are home-centered—when their home has radio, television, phonographs, magazines—bypass the social hierarchy of their community to make direct contact with broader social realities and values. Thus the miner in the north of France, socially and culturally isolated, establishes, thanks to his television set, a direct contact with the entire world, far beyond the traditional forms of social and cultural participation of the urban middle class.

As soon as we begin to consider a highly evolved industrial civilization in which the traditional professional and social sources of culture have been in great part destroyed and in which cultural activity is defined as the level of participation in values worked out centrally and no longer on the level of individual lived experience—just as work is determined by a technical organization and no longer by the professional experience of the worker—attachment to cultural values that are bound to one's trade and primary social groups is no longer an "active" and creative attitude but rather the expression of weak participation in the social sources of culture.

In this situation, "passive" submission to the mass media is an impoverished but positive form of contact with cultural values. A choice between returning to traditional cultural themes and memberships or the passive consumption of the mass media does not exist. These are two closely connected manifestations of cultural underdevelopment, which is itself bound to the weak participation of the masses in the values and products of technical civilization and social democracy. Therefore, we must replace an analysis that starts from the individual and the psychological functions of leisure activity with a more sociological analysis that first of all considers what kind of relations exist within a society, a social class, or an age category, between individuals and the cultural themes that characterize their overall society.

As we have said, it is indispensable at the outset to sort out leisure activities and to distinguish the various functions that they fulfill. But once this preliminary work is done, it is dangerous to carry on the analysis with the help of ideas that relate purely to individual psychology. Since leisure activities are such a socially and historically defined object of study, it is almost inevitable that the psychological notions used will be full of social presuppositions.

It is not only justifiable but indispensable to inquire into the effects of disjointed piecework on leisure behavior; sociologists and psychologists, psychiatrists and psychoanalysts will work together to great advantage, as the analyses of Erich Fromm and Friedmann demonstrate. But this study of the psychological processes must not be confused with the definition of the situation in which they develop. Unless these two points of view are clearly separated, one risks suggesting that industrial civilization destroys some earlier harmony and balance. While we have said that industrialization ruins the traditional bonds of professional experience, socio-professional roles, and cultural orientations, we do not think for a moment that preindustrial societies or those at the beginnings of industrialization are more favorable to cultural initiative.

More practically, it is dangerous to connect the consumption of mass leisure activities too exclusively to piecework, since the workers most directly subject to this kind of work do not seem to be the principal consumers of mass leisure activities. Only on the basis of a sociological definition of the situation under consideration can one profitably utilize notions that refer to individual or even social psychology for the study of behavior that develops in this situation. The expressions *active leisure* and *passive leisure* seem to us dangerous to the degree that they favor the confusion of two analytical levels and insinuate that the passive leisure activities born of modern techniques are opposed to traditional, individual, active leisure activities. They surreptitiously introduce the myth of a harmonious and balanced preindustrial civilization.

We must go further. Does not the development of mass culture increase freedom of choice by subjecting producers to the increasingly varied tastes of the public instead of cultural values much more closely tied to the established social order? By the same token, it could be reasonably said that the mass production organizations, quite varied and subject to increasingly rapid change, are less restrictive for their members than firms of the old type in which a hierarchized and very concentrated authority limited the influence of the much greater number. The least advanced industrial societies are most authoritarian and bureaucratic. As demands diversify in the cultural order, do not the constraints exercised by the producers become attenuated?

These observations are correct on condition that we add that this freedom of initiative and this capacity to exert influence are progressively more unequally distributed among the various professional and social levels. We must recognize that initiative can only exist at the top of society, while the middle levels are dominated by imitative behavior, and the lower levels by withdrawal or subordination to the spectacles organized by the social elite. In another sense, this reintroduces the distinction between active and passive leisure activities or, if one prefers, between elite and mass culture. This cultural stratification can be somewhat balanced by strong social mobility that dilutes the exclusive influence of background. But this compensation becomes less and less sufficient, for today the upper levels define themselves less by property or money than by education and managerial roles, that is, by cultural characteristics. This creates cultural barriers that are more difficult to breach than economic barriers. Above all, the very existence of mass consumption allows much more potent diffusion of behavior and tastes which strengthen the control of the dominant classes and the ruling groups.

These two series of observations are not contradictory. Mass society on one side appears hierarchized and subjected to increasingly powerful forces of cultural manipulation, and on the other side as a kind of social organization in which the individual's freedom of movement and choice is more and more important so that an increasing number of its members can escape some of the influences exercised over them and can act autonomously. But does this not mean that participation is increasingly dominated and that withdrawal is more and more common and can lead to the formation of new life-styles that are foreign to the mass society, new subcultures to which a rich society permits broad possibilities? Perhaps this is the situation meant by the word *leisure*.

Cultural behavior is determined by both propaganda and social level. But the individual's increasingly specific and limited roles within groups to which he belongs allow long periods for the satisfaction of personal tastes. This permits a certain withdrawal from the constraints of social life. The more the duration of work is reduced, the more this area of socially unregulated behavior will be increased. According to the level of one's education and income, it will be dedicated to activities of relaxation or to getting away from social and cultural pressures by escape either in space or in time.

The social stratification of leisure activities can be summed up in this way: on the lowest level are those who have the lowest income and remain locked into marginal zones marked by the decay of earlier cultural worlds—immigrant workers from culturally different countries or regions, workers in declining industries, the aged, low-scale wage earners who try to protect themselves by maintaining family bonds. Above them, there is the large number of production workers who do not participate in the mass culture except by their acquisition of products and their consumption of spectacles and who protect themselves by withdrawal into primary groups. Above them, there are those whose work is defined by a function and rank in an organization. This group is the most open to the influence of clearly hierarchized cultural messages. For this group, promotion, mobility, and the imitation of the higher groups are essential objectives. Finally, at the top, those who perform tasks connected with management or knowledge and have no great "status anxiety" cultivate an aristocratic style of life: cultural activity for its own sake, freedom to move in time and space, an interest in searching for new cultural experiences.

This quick sketch shows at least that the convenient expression *mass culture* means neither the equalization of cultural consumption nor the formation of a universe of leisure activity independent from professional activity. Like leisure activities, consumer activities are more and more socially labeled; innovation is increasingly concentrated at the top. This cultural integration is not necessarily restrictive. It becomes so only if a strongly centralized political power acting according to an explicit ideology governs all cultural production. When this is not the case, an increasing number of individuals have the possibility of withdrawal, escape, or autonomous choice, that is, they can form new elective groups. This constitutes the essence of what we call leisure and is why, in rich societies, individuals who are questioned generally feel themselves "free." But the essential fact is that cultural activity is determined by the level of social participation, by the place occupied on the ladder of stratification.

This lends itself to a very classic insight. Those with weak professional, economic, and social participation are turned in on primary groups based on kinship, neighborhood, or work, and view the broader society as a spectacle brought into their homes by words and pictures. More active leisure activities develop to the degree that the level of social participation is raised, which quite simply reflects the conclusion of the statisticians: to the degree that the standard of living is raised, the portion of the budget that can be used for elective, personalized activities that are relatively liberated from the needs of elementary subsistence increases more than proportionately.

Work and Leisure
in French Sociology

JOFFRE DUMAZEDIER
AND NICOLE LATOUCHE*

Much less is known about the contours of leisure in our own day than many people think. As Dumazedier and Latouche, two French sociologists who have studied the question point out in the following article, it is only recently that the matter has been investigated systematically. The authors draw upon a number of national and local studies of leisure which have been conducted in France; they are interested in the extent of leisure in the society as a whole, the content of leisure, and the variations in both of these by social class. Basically optimistic about the conclusions which they draw from these studies, they suggest several policy implications for governments to explore. Readers who

SOURCE: Joffre Dumazedier and Nicole Latouche, "Work and Leisure in French Sociology," *Industrial Relations* 1 (1962): 13–30. Reprinted by permission of the authors and publishers.

*Joffre Dumazedier and Nicole Latouche are associated with the Centre d'études Sociologiques, Paris. The article was translated by Edward Geiger.

have sensed the ironical mood of de Grazia as he described the emergence of modern forms of popular amusement, or who have followed the complex formulations of Touraine's critique, might well prefer a sharper critical edge to the evaluation of contemporary leisure life. But such a judgment requires detailed information, and this can only come from future research which the authors propose.

In France, as in all European countries, the sociology of leisure is new. When Veblen published his *Theory of the Leisure Class* (1898) in the United States, Durkheim in France had only recently published his essay on the division of labor (1893) and was preparing his course on education.[1] In his essay, Durkheim barely outlined a connection between work and leisure. To the extent that it was touched upon, the discussion concerned spontaneous personal relations of a type which, off the job, would prolong the effects of the division of labor and continue the solidarity which had been created: "The real function of the division of labor is to create a feeling of solidarity between two or more persons. In whatever manner this result is obtained, it is the division of labor which gives birth to these groups of friends and marks them with its imprint."[2]

In the same work, Durkheim did not seem to take into account the worker's aspirations, which had been discussed ten years earlier in a pamphlet on the "right to laziness" by Paul Lafargue.[3] Durkheim believed that the activity of playing had a negative influence in the realm of social obligations. "The need to play, to act without any goal and simply for

1. E. Durkheim, "L'évolution et le rôle de l'Enseignement secondaire en France," the *Revue Politique et Littéraire* and the *Revue Scientifique,* 20 (January 1906).

2. E. Durkheim, *De la division du travail social* (Paris: F. Alcan, 1893), p. 57.

3. P. Lafargue, *Le Droit à la Paresse* (1893).

pleasure, cannot be developed beyond a certain point without interfering with the serious side of life."[4] On the other hand, education for him concerned only compulsory schooling for children. It excluded the newer forms of adult education which had been stimulated by the movement toward organization of leisure at the end of the last century: sports associations, lecture societies, university extension courses, and the like.

However, before the time of Durkheim, French philosophers had emphasized the necessity either of a continuous development in relation to one's occupational life or of periodic self-improvement integrated with one's leisure-time activity. Comte viewed education as gradual and continuous preparation of the man. A contemporary philosopher who analyzed this aspect of Comte's work concluded that, for Comte, "the concept of education covers the whole of life" and "the education of the adult . . . is not complementary but formative."[5]

In 1933, in the new edition of his study of working-class needs, Halbwachs noted the degrading influence of industrial work on certain off-the-job activities, particularly family and social activities. "If the feeling for the family is weakening, the surest sign of it is that men . . . are satisfied to spend their time, in the intervals between their working hours, in environments where social life is more relaxed, more dissipated, and as if coarsened by the influence of mechanical forces in the surroundings."[6]

But it was Georges Friedmann who posed the problem of

4. Durkheim, *De la division . . .* , p. 263.

5. A. Bastide, *La doctrine de l'Education Universelle dans la philosophie d'A. Comte* (Paris: P.U.F., 1957), vol. 2, p. 403. See also, Proudhon, *De la justice dans la Révolution et dans l'Eglise, Sixième étude: le travail* (Brussels: A. Schnée, 1860), p. 98.

6. M. Halbwachs, *La classe ouvrière et les niveaux de vie* (Paris: F. Alcan, 1912), pp. 446–447.

the *relation between work and leisure as such* for the first time in France. The relation between these two activities takes a central place among "the human problems of mechanization"; it is a major aspect of this "giant experiment with uncertain results" which the coming of technical civilization constitutes for man.[7] Friedmann suggested at first that the progress of the division and mechanization of labor results in a loss of interest on the part of the worker and that leisure becomes not only a distraction but a compensation. With the progress of empirical work, his theory became more refined. In the preface to a recent study of pigeon cultivation among miners, he drew some general reflections from the detailed data.[8] Leisure, he pointed out, does more than merely offer a compensation for the technique of work. In the example of pigeon cultivation it brings different compensations: "professional compensations for work with a limited horizon, emotional compensations for the crudity of social relations in a mass of people, social compensations through the success which this leisure-time activity can provide." Finally, far from being a compensation, leisure is more often only an extension of occupational life. Louchet's study shows that there is a tendency for the most frustrating leisure to be associated with the most frustrating work. However, in the case of the pigeon cultivators, the intellectual level and quality of training introduce a new type of conditioning. "Better trained intellectually, [they] can participate more fully in discussions and in the organization of meetings."

Marxist thought as a whole has been greatly concerned with work and little interested in leisure. Leisure under the

7. G. Friedmann, *Problèmes humains du machinisme industriel* (Paris: Gallimard, 1946), p. 372.

8. Preface by G. Friedmann in *La colombophilie chez les mineurs du nord*, Jacqueline Frish-Gauthier and P. Louchet (Paris: CNRS, 1961), pp. vi–vii.

capitalist system is viewed as a source of escape from the exigencies of the struggles for liberation. However, two unorthodox Marxist sociologists have in different ways outlined another approach to the relations between work and nonwork. For Lefebvre, leisure not only can be studied as a threat to the class struggle, it is also an ambiguous but positive fact of contemporary life. It is evidence of a new aspiration of all classes for happiness.[9] For Naville, leisure is not just a means of duplicating the satisfactions of work. It has a value of its own. The author adds a remark, the elaboration of which we await with interest: "With the extension of free time, work and nonwork both are beginning to change their meaning."[10] What will become of the Marxist notion of work at the end of this analysis?

It is especially among young industrial sociologists, colleagues of Georges Friedmann, that leisure has become a subject of empirical studies oriented toward a better understanding of the evolution of the real attitudes of industrial workers, particularly in the work situation. Thus, at the end of a study of the Renault factories, Touraine wrote: "The problem of leisure poses itself in this setting in a new manner, no longer as research into compensations but as an integral part, in the same sense as work, of the social system."[11] According to him, the content of the worker's leisure is rooted less and less in a direct occupational and social experience; it is more and more determined by a mass culture centrally elaborated and diffused throughout society. Certainly working-class life has special characteristics; this is borne out by the results of Chombart de Lauwe's anthropological investigations of working-class families in Paris, Bor-

9. H. Lefebvre, *Critique de la vie quotidienne* (Paris: L'Arche, 1958).

10. P. Naville, *De l'aliénation à la jouissance* (Paris: Marcel Rivière, 1957), p. 497.

11. A. Touraine, *L'évolution du travail ouvrier aux usines Renault* (Paris: CNRS, 1955), p. 181.

deaux, and Nantes.[12] But these characteristics frequently are only reflections of the inequalities that survive as a result of economic and cultural disparities. Through his studies of a population of white-collar workers, Crozier arrives at similar conclusions. What he calls "the cultural levels of leisure" play an important role in the ambiguity of the social conscience of white-collar workers. Economically their environment resembles that of the wage earners, but culturally they aspire to the environment of the managerial class.[13]

It is in the context of this evolution of the sociology of work that the group concerned with the sociology of leisure and popular culture (founded in 1953) began its research. This research is focused on leisure itself. It is directed less toward activities than toward the structure of the cultural and social content of these activities. Such content is studied in its reciprocal relations not only with work but also with the whole set of extraoccupational obligations: family, civic, and so on.[14] Our central hypothesis is that the norms and values of leisure of the masses have general implications in the development of society and culture. The study of the effects of these norms and values on the participation of the masses in occupational, familial, or social responsibility and in technical, artistic, and scientific endeavor appears to us the most important task for research.

Let us make quite clear the point of view we have adopted. We think that the sociology of leisure must pay particular attention to study of the cultural development of the masses, according to various clearly specified criteria. The studies should be not only critical but constructive. As leisure displays changes, both quantitative and qualitative, the soci-

12. P. H. Chombart de Lauwe, *La vie quotidienne des familles ouvrières* (Paris: CNRS, 1956).

13. M. Crozier, *Petits fonctionnaires au travail* (Paris: CNRS, 1955).

14. J. Dumazedier, "Problèmes actuels de la sociologie du loisir," *UNESCO International Bulletin of Social Sciences* 4 (1960).

ology of leisure should equip itself to formulate in objective terms the various alternatives which are available for social decision. It should be prepared to illuminate the social and cultural implications of these choices. This sociology would be both suggestive and predictive without, however, being at all prescriptive. Just as economics tends to become the science of coordinated and planned economic development, so sociology should attempt to constitute in one science the alternatives of free and spontaneous or planned cultural development.[15] It is a difficult task. It is also the most effective way in which the sociology of leisure can contribute to the progress of social and cultural democracy. It is in this perspective that we shall attempt to analyze the relations between work and leisure with the data we have available at present.[16]

Leisure and Socioeconomic Alternatives

There are people who think that leisure in the everyday life of the masses will automatically increase, thanks to the discovery of new sources of energy and of automation. Thus in both capitalist and socialist societies hours of work will decline, resulting in the disappearance of former social disparities. We shall leave the era of work and enter the "era of

15. In France, for the first time (February 1961), a study commission on cultural action assembled, under the auspices of the Commissariat au Plan d'équipement et de modernisation, sociologists, economists, and those responsible for the dissemination of information (film, press, radio, and television) relating to cultural stimulation and adult education.

16. We will use, in the first place, the results of research carried out by the group on the sociology of leisure and popular culture of the Centre d'Études Sociologiques, especially a historical study of the evolution of leisure since 1830. Other studies which will be utilized deal with the representation of leisure (limits and functions) in a representative sample of 819 wage earners and low-salaried urban employees (1953) and with leisure in the development of an industrial agglomeration, Annecy (50,000 inhabitants), carried out in 1957 and now being analyzed. In addition, various other research results in industrial sociology will also be utilized.

leisure." This prophecy of poets and technocrats poses the question of the actual relations between the development of leisure, technical progress, and social decision.

Certainly leisure in itself is a product of industrial civilization. Through mechanization, concentration, and increasing division and organization of productive processes, a more distinct time for work, as opposed to time off the job, is created. Developing its productive capacity, technical civilization increases its free time, while augmenting the productivity of time spent at work. In France, the average workweek has declined from seventy-five hours to forty-five hours in a century. Today an urban worker disposes of about twenty to thirty hours of leisure or semileisure a week[17] and of a minimum of three weeks of paid vacation a year. Thus it is likely that the discovery of new sources of energy and the extension of automation will result in an increase in free time; in this sense, it is valid to take the position that leisure is continually being created by technical progress.

But it is not created automatically; the increase in free time and diminution of working time are part of the social progress which has come about through a continuous struggle between opposed interests. Naville remarked that at the beginning of the century the sudden development of machines should have automatically resulted in a decline in hours of work. However, nothing happened because the workers did not have the power to insist on it. On the other hand, in 1936 a new relation between employer and union forces, stimulated by the fear of an increase in unemployment, resulted in the sudden achievement of twelve days of paid vacation and a forty-hour week. But the country was

17. Estimated on the basis of our Annecy study and the studies of Chombart de Lauwe, *La vie quotidienne* . . . ; of J. Fourastie, *Machinisme et bien-être* (Paris: de Minuit, 1951); and of J. Stoetzel, *Renouveau des idées sur la famille* (Cahiers de l'Ined, 1954).

later forced to give up the forty-hour week, not only because of the circumstances of the war but also because the productive capacity of industry at that time could not support such a reduction of work without a stagnation of the standard of living.[18] Thus the increase in leisure under the influence of technical progress depends also on current social forces and the choices made as to the direction of productive effort. What is the outlook? What is the probable future trend in the growth of leisure? What, in this perspective, will be the alternatives available for social decision?

Since 1950, France has entered a phase of economic expansion which the recent recession does not appear to have stopped. In six years, average consumption has increased 36 percent, taking into account the variations in the purchasing power of the franc.[19] However, in 1956, in the midst of a period of expansion, the following question was asked: "Has your level of living improved since a year ago?"[20] Of the salaried population of cities with more than 5,000 inhabitants, only 8 percent answered, "yes, it has increased"; 29 percent said, "no, it has decreased"; and 63 percent, "no, it has neither increased nor decreased."

In the France of today, the gap between the salary received and the salary desired and between the increase of wants and the increase in income is such that the desire to earn more money is probably stronger in the majority of social classes than the desire to have more free time. But the question has not yet been posed in this form. In a recent study, Swedish workers were asked whether they would prefer to have fewer hours of obligatory work, even if this meant

18. Preface by A. Sauvy in *Vue sur l'économie,* Bernard (Cahiers de l'Ined, 1960).

19. G. Rottier, "Loisir, vacances, culture, transfers: analyse par catégories socio-professionnelles," Annals of the Centre de Recherche et de Documentation, in *Consommation* (January–March 1958).

20. "Conditions, attitudes, et aspirations des ouvriers," Institut français d'opinion publique, *Sondages* 2 (1956).

a corresponding decrease in earnings; 60 percent expressed a preference for a decrease in legal hours of work and an increase in leisure time. At what level of living would the French give the same answer? Above all, the needs of the nation determine the amount of work required to bring about an increase in the level of living of the various social classes, aid for underdeveloped countries, defense policy, national prestige, etc. But in a democracy the desires of workers cannot be ignored. At each stage of economic development, sociology should contribute to analyzing the optimum relationships between the need for leisure and the need for money among the various social classes. Such are the terms of the first socioeconomic alternative.

When a decision is made to reduce hours of work, three things can happen. The development of one can, in fact if not in law, operate to the detriment of the others. A decrease in the total number of hours of work can involve a lengthening of obligatory schooling for children, a lowering of the age of retirement for elderly workers, or an increase in leisure for active workers.[21]

Education can be considered "social leisure for the profit of the young."[22] There is a general tendency toward an increase in the period of schooling. In France, a law extending

21. It would be equally important to pose the problem of household work in relation to occupational work. According to a study of the time schedules of married women made by the Institut national d'études démographiques, J. Daric and J. Dayre have calculated that in 1956, out of 105 billion hours of work completed by the entire French population, household work represented about 45 billion. If one considers the fact that women who pursue an occupation work as much at home as outside, i.e., from 77 to 84 hours a week, according to the number of children, one can envisage another alternative: to what extent should time freed from occupational work result in an increase in leisure for the man or to diminution of household work for the woman? See J. Dumazedier and M. F. Lanfant, *Rapport introductif à la Commission "Famille loisir" du séminaire européen sur la politique sociale face à l'évolution des besoins de la famille,* Office des affaires sociales de l'O.N.U. (Arnheim, Holland, April 1961).

22. P. Ducassé, "Science, technique, et loisir," *Impact* 1 (1952).

compulsory education to age sixteen was adopted in 1961. But Fourastie shows that an increase of two hours per week in leisure time for 30,000,000 adults corresponds, in its effects on the economy, to an increase of approximately a year in school for French youth.[23]

According to a study conducted among persons aged sixty to seventy in the Paris region, who were retired a year ago, half continued to work in normal employment, but almost half applied for a pension before age sixty-five. Among 100 reasons for stopping work, "fatigue" was most often mentioned. Shouldn't the age of retirement be made more flexible to permit some to continue working while others enter the leisure of retirement before age sixty-five?[24]

Finally, research indicates that a forty-hour week is considered the ideal workweek by more than half of wage earners, white-collar workers, and managerial workers.[25] Furthermore, progress in the scientific organization of work has frequently led to accentuated fatigue, and a forty-hour week has again become an actual subject of union demands. The continuous working day meets major resistance in France, in spite of the advantage of leisure at the end of the afternoon; on the other hand, the feeling in favor of free time over the weekend is gaining ground from year to year. The week with "two Sundays" seems preferred, even if, in compensation, the working day must last nine or ten hours. Since August 1956, the legal length of the paid annual vacation for all categories of workers has been three weeks. Already investi-

23. J. Fourastie, *La civilisation de 1975* (Paris: P.U.F., 1957), p. 70.

24. See J. Daric, "Vicillisement de la population et prolongation de la vie active," *Travaux et Documents* 7 (1948).

25. In reply to the question, "What is the length of the ideal workweek?" the replies were: forty hours—54 percent of the wage earners, 56 percent of the salaried workers, and 54 percent of the management personnel, *Sondages* 2 (1956).

gations have indicated that the desire to have a month's vacation is shared by 49 percent of wage earners, 82 percent of white-collar workers, and 56 percent of managerial workers.[26] A law on cultural vacations adopted in 1957 introduced a new type of vacation of twelve unpaid days for all workers who wished to pursue a union educational program. A combination of union, cultural, and educational forces is now exerting pressure on the government, parliament, and public opinion to extend this law to all sorts of training and improvement programs.

It appears, then, that an increase in leisure in the coming years will involve choices between complex alternatives, and, furthermore, the national interest may be in conflict with the aspirations of various classes and groups. The Commissariat for Planning anticipates that between now and 1965 there will be a decline of only about one hour in actual effective working time.

It must be emphasized that the extension of leisure certainly depends on technical progress, but it does not depend on that alone. The hailing of the "era of leisure" as an automatic consequence of automation is a new form of what Friedmann calls "technical utopianism."[27] Leisure results both from the possibilities offered by technical progress and the conscious or unconscious socioeconomic choices of the nation and of the classes and social groups of which the nation is composed. Leisure is above all, under the combined impact of technical progress and social decision, time freed by productive work in favor of unproductive activity of man. Technical progress merely fixes the limits within which social choices can be made.

26. "Conditions, attitudes, et aspirations des ouvriers," Institut français d'opinion publique, *Sondages* 2 (1956): 34.

27. G. Friedmann, *Le travail en miettes* (Paris: Gallimard, 1956).

Leisure and Sociocultural Alternatives

Socioeconomic developments have their cultural implications. It is insufficient to maintain that leisure results in the development of a "fun morality" or the love of hobbies. "Fun morality" and hobbies have different meanings in the culture of the masses. These cultural differences are what seem important to us to study. What encourages or discourages the expansion of the personality in social obligations and cultural activities? Such a question puts us on the road toward formulating criteria for analysis of the content of leisure.

Let us first specify the limits within which these criteria can be formulated and applied:

1. Leisure is not all time which is free from work. It occupies only a part—that part which does not involve any legal or moral obligation.[28] Even when it arises from social pressure (conformity, snobbishness), it is distinguished from the primary obligations imposed by the basic institutions of society. In about 60 percent of the responses to a nationwide inquiry it was differentiated from work; in 40 percent it was differentiated from other primary obligations: family, civic, spiritual.

2. The dominant character of the relations between leisure and primary obligations is *opposition*. Voluntary prolongation of the activities or preoccupations of work into leisure time was noted only in a small number of cases.

3. *Work-obligation* is that work which takes place after the legal hours of labor. It includes both supplementary work in the firm and complementary work outside the firm, often outside the occupation: 25 percent of the active population of Annecy, as compared with 21 percent of the wage earners, thus prolonged their remunerative work. There must be added to this category that part of domestic work which is imposed by the needs of the family.

4. There is also an important group of activities which, from the point of view of the individual, arise in the first place from leisure, but which represent in differing degrees the character of obligations. We call

28. Here we are using the results of a national study of the representation of leisure (1953), p. 7.

these activities *semileisure.* Their duration can be as long as that of pure leisure.[29]

5. Finally, every leisure-time activity can fulfill several functions according to situations and attitudes: the function of recuperation which frees one from fatigue, the function of diversion which frees one from boredom, and the function of free development which liberates one from routine and makes possible the voluntary growth of physical, intellectual, or social capacities.[30]

Within these limits the contents of leisure can assume varying significance according to our criteria. We have isolated several activities in the form of dichotomies (activities which can be classified into two groups with differing characteristics). They are based on the results of our study of 415 male heads of families in Annecy.

Semileisure activities are usually connected with family life. We have looked both for cases in which family semileisure is looked upon favorably and those in which it is not.

In connection with pure leisure, we have distinguished physical activities which require a sizable effort, such as sport or mountain excursions, and others which require very little, such as walks.

We have similarly treated another group of activities which stimulate the mind, distinguishing (1) simple participation in the amusements of country fairs or festivals and attendance at artistic events, and (2) mental activity limited to reading of the daily newspaper and that which includes the use of books and the desire for cultural vacations.

29. From the point of view of occupational and domestic work, we distinguish four categories of semileisure: (1) leisure activities of a semilucrative, semidisinterested character, such as remunerative odd-job indoor work or participation in orchestras, etc.; (2) domestic activities of a semiutilitarian, semirecreational type, such as gardening or "do-it-yourself"; (3) familial activities of a semidistractive, semieducational nature, such as playing with children; (4) small, agreeable jobs, such as decoration, or making small models of boats, etc. These jobs have more the character of an activity freely chosen for its own sake than of an imposed obligation.

30. J. Dumazedier, "Travail et loisir," in *Traité de Sociologie du travail,* eds. G. Friedmann and P. Naville (Paris: Colin, 1961).

Finally, we have compared patterns of frequenting cafés and of voluntary membership in organizations, as well as spontaneous interest in or indifference toward civic or political activities.

Although these dichotomies are simplified, they are important to the problems of leisure which confront responsible groups concerned with sociocultural action.

We have looked for the relationships between these different aspects of leisure and certain characteristics of working life which can be expected to become more important in the future. These characteristics are related to sociooccupational status, work conditions, and the attitudes of workers. Through our research we believe we can develop reliable indicators of the evolution of leisure activities. Although the condition of "all other things being equal" did not prevail during our study, and in ten years, for example, other more influential factors may influence leisure activities, current social decisions could be made on the basis of better information about predictable developments.[31]

In the period when Karl Marx observed the French proletariat, about 90 percent of all workers were wage earners.[32] According to the latest (1954) figures of the National Institute of Statistical and Economic Studies, in a total labor force of 19.2 million, the number of agricultural employees was 1.2 million (or 6 percent) and that of nonagricultural wage earners was 6.5 million (or 33.8 percent). Since about 65 percent of the French labor force consists of employees, nonagricul-

31. The relationships which we report here yield a chi² that is significant at the 5 percent level. To neutralize the variables which we cannot control, we have utilized the method of matched pairs. This statistical work is in process. Thus the results reported here have only an indicative value which requires confirmation. See the definitive publication, *Travail et Loisir*, in the series *Le loisir et la ville*, by J. Dumazedier and N. Latouche (Paris: CNRS, 1963).

32. *Recensement de 1851*. Urban and rural wage earners, including domestics, constituted 90.1 percent of French employed workers.

tural wage earners thus represent no more than half (50.7 percent) of all employees. Not only has the number of wage earners diminished in relative importance in the last century but their level and style of living has gone through a metamorphosis. In this evolution leisure has increased for the majority of workers in amount and in enticement, prestige, and worth, despite an unfavorable situation for a minority.[33]

Under these conditions what are the actual relations between sociooccupational status and patterns of leisure activity? In France it is particularly interesting to compare wage earners and groups such as salaried employees and middle management, handicraftsmen and small businessmen.[34] Are the cultural similarities more important or less important than the differences? Can one *still* speak of a specific culture of the working class or must one speak of a culture that is common to the principal urban social classes? Finally, in what direction is the content of mass leisure likely to evolve with the decline in the relative number of wage earners and the predictable expansion of the social classes which we shall designate for want of a better term as "middle classes"?

In the first place, most people in all social categories regularly engage in "do-it-yourself" activities. The difference between the proportion of wage earners participating in this type of activity and that of salaried employees is not significant: 75.5 percent as compared with 70.5 percent.[35] How-

33. Friedmann and Naville, eds., *Traité de Sociologie du travail.* . . .

34. In Annecy the proportion of wage earners in the labor force is 34 percent; that of salaried employees, 11 percent; that of middle management, 9 percent; and that of handicraftsmen and small businessmen, 22 percent; totalling 76 percent.

35. Whenever we refer to salaried employees, it will be understood that we generally include salaried employees and middle management; similarly, when we refer to small businessmen, it will be understood that we include handicraftsmen and small businessmen. However, in some instances separate data are reported for middle management and handicraftsmen.

ever, contrary to what was expected, the wage earners were more likely to engage in "do-it-yourself" activities for pleasure (and not for necessity) than was our sample as a whole, but the difference was still slight (40 percent as compared with 30 percent).

Open-air activities, including sports and other quieter activities such as bowling or fishing, interest all social categories. Nevertheless, some slight differences should be mentioned: bowling is less common among salaried employees (22.5 percent) than among wage earners (29 percent). The same difference appears in the case of fishing.

In a city where snow-covered mountains can be reached in less than an hour by auto, skiing interests the working class (17.5 percent) almost as much as small businessmen (18.5 percent) and a little more than salaried workers (14.5 percent). But these differences are not significant. The practice of Sunday motor trips is already comparable among the different classes, but wage earners are still behind salaried employees: 13 percent as compared with 27 percent.[36]

The taste for festivals and shows is equally shared by all social classes, but wage earners go to the movies a little less than salaried employees or small businessmen. One finds the same preferences for movie and singing stars. Going to the theater is infrequent among all groups. And as for reading? Two out of three homes of wage earners have a library as compared with three out of four among salaried employees. The contents of wage earners' libraries are not limited to the dictionary and classical books; they include all types of books with a relative neglect of the more serious books in favor of paperback novels, illustrated novels, and detective stories: 37

36. In Annecy, 17 percent of the heads of wage earner families had autos, as compared with 47 percent of the salaried employees; in France, it is estimated that about one family in four has a car; in the Paris region, almost one in three.

percent have these latter types as compared with 12 percent of the libraries of salaried employees and 14 percent of the libraries of small businessmen.

One finds the same type of pattern in connection with participation in associations. Among wage earners, 44 percent of family heads belong to an association as compared with 60 percent of salaried employees and 58 percent of middle management. This difference is even more pronounced in regard to taking responsibility for the running of the organizations: 8 percent of wage earners as compared with 17 percent of handicraftsmen and 35 percent of middle management exercise responsibility in an organization. Finally, there is a difference in participation in cultural life: only 4 percent of wage earners who are members of associations belong to a cultural organization (music, painting, literature, or conferences), compared with 16 percent of small businessmen and handicraftsmen and 20 percent of salaried employees.

Thus the values and norms of leisure do not seem to us to be radically different. We have not found a tendency for wage earners to reject the norms of leisure of certain other social groups. The content of leisure is already common to all social categories to a considerable extent, but there are still quantitative and qualitative differences between wage earners and other groups. Some of the differences we have not mentioned, for example, a taste for simplicity, correspond to values which are perhaps specifically in the working-class tradition. Most of them correspond to differences in participation in social and cultural life which are likely to decrease as the general level of living rises and as the rise in the level of education becomes more pronounced for everyone. This evolution will take place all the more rapidly as the movement for prolonging schooling and extending permanent education for adults, accompanied by a policy of cultural vacations, continues to develop.

Differences in sociooccupational status are probably the strongest influence on norms and values of leisure. But this is not the only influence. We shall consider two others: the modernization of enterprises and associated changes in social activities. Both seem to be part of an irreversible movement which has been growing and which is likely to be still more pronounced in the years to come. When an enterprise is modernized or becomes more social, the character of industrial life tends to change. What are the consequences for leisure? In what direction is the content of leisure of the workers likely to evolve?

Modern enterprises of recent construction reflect preoccupation with hygiene, comfort, and esthetic qualities which create a different environment for work from that of the old factory. One wonders sometimes whether it is not just a difference in degree but a difference in kind. At Annecy, a factory built after 1945 resembles an administrative building or a modern school more than enterprises in the same industry built more than fifty years ago. In a study of three firms in a valley in the South of France, Moscovici had already observed that participation in a modern enterprise results in more pronounced changes in the attitudes of workers coming from rural areas than does participation in traditional enterprises. It is in the most modern enterprise that the feeling of being deprived of "distraction and vacations" is most pronounced (22 percent as compared with 7 percent in traditional firms).[37]

What are the significant connections between the type of enterprise in which the worker is employed (modern or old-fashioned) and the leisure-time activities of workers? Participation in the semileisure activities of the family is distributed in the same way in the two populations. On the other hand, participation in activities outside the family, such as sports,

37. S. Moscovici, *La reconversion industrielle et les changements sociaux* (Paris: Colin, 1961).

especially mountain sport, are clearly more pronounced among the workers in the most modern factories. Although participation in local festivals is relatively frequent in both groups, the workers in the older factories prefer religious festivals. Interest in political life is equal in the two groups, but it is expressed in different ways. Workers in the modern factories show their interest to a greater extent through reading the headlines in the newspapers, whereas the others tend to attach more importance to political conversations in cafés. With respect to social life, workers in the older factories are more interested in the "serious" aspects of daily life as exemplified by their greater tendency to discuss the work situation during time passed in the café, whereas the workers of the more modernized factories liberate themselves more effectively from work and discuss inconsequential subjects "by fits and starts" at the café.

When they show a desire to benefit from cultural vacations, workers in the traditional factories are more likely to choose programs of a general cultural type. Finally, in the domain of intellectual activities, we find that the workers who participate in the life of a modern factory tend to prefer discussions of actual problems, as indicated by their preference for reports in the newspapers.

Whether firms are modern or old-fashioned, they often have varied social activities. The social role of the firm has been enlarging since the beginning of the century, and it is probable that this role will continue to develop in the future, whatever the economic and political context. Does participation in an enterprise with an active program result in a particular pattern of leisure activity?

In Annecy, among thirty firms with more than fifty employees,[38] eight have a Comité d'Entreprise, managed more or less democratically, which assumes responsibility for social

38. Of which there were one with more than 2,000 and six with more than 200 employees.

projects, including the organization of leisure-time activity for both the workers and their families (sports, vacation camps, organized trips, etc.).[39] We were not surprised to find that the personnel of factories with an active Comité d'Entreprise tended to spend their vacations away from parents or grandparents and were less likely to engage in "do-it-yourself" activities during vacations. We did not find open-air activities significantly popular among the personnel of such factories.

The personnel of social factories tended to have lively curiosities. They were more likely to visit expositions with a utilitarian character and benefited more from company libraries. They read more books, particularly detective stories. Workers of other enterprises were more likely to choose classical books, novels, and scientific magazines. Desire for education in social responsibilities was more marked in firms which had the most highly developed social programs; the desire for technical training, with a view to ensuring promotion, was more developed in the other enterprises. The tendency to participate in a more active social life was accompanied by stronger adhesion to union organization and by a more marked interest in political activity.

Thus, differences in status or situation are reflected in differences in the content of leisure. Is it the same with regard to differences in attitudes toward work? It is known that technical progress has reduced physical fatigue but increased boredom. However, in Annecy, in all firms, small and large, industrial, commercial, and administrative, only 15.8 per-

39. In France, a law of 1946 requires all industrial and commercial firms with more than fifty employees to set up a Comité d'Entreprise elected by all categories of personnel. This committee must administer all social projects. However, of 20,000 firms subject to the law, about 10,000 have a committee. Scarcely 3,500 have one which actually functions. See Montuclard, "Pour une Sociologie de la participation ouvrière dans les comités d'entreprise," *Revue de sociologie du travail* (October–December 1960).

cent of the employees looked upon their work as without interest, or boring. It is known, also, that in all types of industrial societies more or less effective efforts are made to interest workers in their jobs by varied methods, e.g., decor, job enlargement, financial autonomy of departments, democratizing the organization, social projects, codetermination, etc. How is leisure affected when the level of satisfaction in work is raised?

We have compared the responses of those who have an interest in their work and those who do not. The attitudes expressed are not particularly different among those who engage in "do-it-yourself" activities, sports, and festivals. One observes a slight tendency for the worker who expresses satisfaction with his work to attach less importance to certain semileisure activities which are centered in the home, such as family festivals. Further, one observes in this group a more definite attitude with regard to certain kinds of festivals, such as country fairs; they are either accepted or rejected.

On the other hand, it is in connection with informative and self-improvement activities that the most significant differences appear. It is among the workers who find their work interesting that intellectual curiosity and the need for complementary education are most lively. They read more serials and literary novels. They show more desire to participate in cultural vacations aimed at general culture or preparation for social responsibilities. Indeed, those who are particularly satisfied with their work tend to assume more responsibilities, such as administrative or technical leadership in associations of all kinds,[40] except, however, in political action groups where more workers who are not interested in their professional work are found.

40. These conclusions are similar to those of Crozier and Motta in their research, *Le personnel d'une compagnie d'assurances* (Paris: ISST, 1956), and to those of Gauthier and Louchet, *La colombophilie. . . .*

Thus, lack of satisfaction with work does not seem to be linked to particularly active intellectual or social leisure-time activities (if we leave aside the ambivalent case of political pursuits). It appears, on the contrary, that intellectual and social leisure-time activities are related to a manifest interest in work.

Whether satisfied or not with their work, some persons used part of their free time to improve themselves in their occupations, while others remained indifferent to promotion. In France, during the last decade, programs of firms and universities aimed at stimulating improvement of technical management have sharply expanded.[41] These programs, according to the experts, will assume an even more important place in the firms of tomorrow. Furthermore, according to certain authors, attitudes toward professional promotion will probably have a more important impact on the mentality of the workers concerned than on the norms of the class to which they belong.[42] We were thus very much interested in the possible relationship between a positive attitude to occupational improvement and patterns of leisure-time activities.[43] There was none for "do-it-yourself" family activities, walks or sports, festivals or spectacles. On the other hand, interest in serious magazines like *Science et Vie* and faithful attendance at conferences or study clubs were, as one might have expected, more frequent among those who were per-

41. The shortage of management personnel, and especially of middle management, is still very acute. Experts of the Commissariat du Plan have recently estimated the shortage at about one million for France as a whole, which included about 500,000 industrial management personnel in 1954 (or about 10 percent of all wage earners).

42. H. Wilensky, "Travail, carrière, et intégration sociale," *UNESCO International Bulletin of Social Sciences* 4 (1960).

43. At Annecy, 43 percent of the active workers said they had never attempted to improve themselves in their trade. Among those who had made this effort, 54 percent had followed more or less systematic training (either reading specialized books or taking a course).

fecting themselves in their occupations. It is very interesting to observe that concern over occupational promotion does not reduce but probably enlarges the general curiosity of the individual. In fact, those who were interested in promotion belonged, in larger numbers, to cultural associations. Finally, their sociability did not seem to be restricted to the firm. They went relatively frequently to cafés, for example, particularly to discuss work, and were more likely to assume responsibilities in the running of associations.

Another set of attitudes, important to the study of workers, concerns participation in union life. To be sure, in France, scarcely 25 percent of the employed are unionized,[44] and the number of individual workdays lost by strikes has declined, according to statistics from the Ministry of Labor, from 22.7 million in 1947 to 4.1 million in 1957. Nevertheless, from a national point of view, the prestige of union leaders depends to a large extent on the annual wage demands, while it has become weaker in political action.[45] All these facts are confirmed in the Annecy study, where the proportion of union members corresponds closely to the French average. Following the same procedure as in other parts of our study, we examined the leisure activities of the unionized and the nonunionized.

Once more we found that in connection with semileisure and open-air activities, the differences were not significant. It was in connection with attendance at certain events that differences began to appear: workers who were not affiliated with a union tended to go to the movies more often (the difference was significant among those who went more than

44. In 1955 there were approximately 2,873,000 workers affiliated with the Syndicat CGT (Communist influence), 1,396,000 affiliated with the Syndicat CFTC (Christian-Democratic influence), and 1,081,000 with the Syndicat FO (Socialist influence).

45. A. Touraine, "Le syndicalisme de contrôle," *Cahiers Internationaux de Sociologie* 7 (1960): 57–88.

five times a year). The unaffiliated were also more interested
in big technical expositions such as the "Salon de l'Automobile."

But it was in connection with informative leisure and social
activities that very marked differences showed up. When
nonunionized workers expressed a desire to benefit from
cultural vacations, their aspirations were centered on programs of occupational training with a view to promotion and
not on preparation for social responsibilities which were unrelated to their occupations.

For their part, unionized workers had more extensive intellectual curiosity. Despite the time passed in meetings,
they were interested in books. It was they who had more
completely equipped personal libraries: more than half of
them owned over seventy-five books. They were also very
interested in reading newspapers and weekly magazines,
where their choice tended more than among the nonunionized toward articles concerned with domestic and foreign
policy.

This latter attitude is also confirmed by the fact that in
Annecy people who participate in political life are recruited
to a greater extent among union members. Finally, although
unionists are more likely to participate in organized groups,
as might be expected, they are relatively indifferent to the
more traditional types of groups: those which are organized
on an age or regional basis.

Conclusion

Thus the decrease in hours of work which has accompanied, and will continue to accompany, increased productivity poses the question of the distribution of leisure time
and the most favorable development of the relationship between work and leisure. At each stage in this evolution, several developments seem probable, while several alternatives

are possible. The social and cultural implications of these choices are of great importance to the masses. Conscious or unconscious choices should not result solely from the more or less blind game of social forces or the calculations of economists alone. The social decisions of governments, parties, unions, and management should be informed on the basis of a sociology of leisure that is cautious and determined to be tentative and predictive.

Can we predict that, in the near future, the leisure activities of the masses will be determined exclusively by the central culture which society spreads among all social classes through the schools or the mass media? Or will the direct experience of the work situation continue to exert an influence on the off-the-job culture of social groups? The first results of our research in France lead us to give a positive answer to this second question. We have found that differences in status, environment, and attitudes linked to work are related to disparities in the cultural and social levels of leisure. These disparities tend to reduce the class consciousness inherited from the nineteenth century; they influence new types of group consciousness, more limited but more dynamic.

To what extent can we be pessimistic or optimistic about the future of the cultural and social level of the leisure of the masses? In the long run, a conditional optimism appears reasonable to us. If changes in the position of the working classes continue, if firms continue to be modernized and to develop their sociocultural programs, if reforms which increase interest in work actively continue, accompanied by stimulation of occupational self-improvement and union educational programs in the midst of the work environment, one can reasonably predict an elevation of the sociocultural level of leisure of an increasing number of workers. On the other hand, without an expansion and intensification of these convergent developments, it would be vain to hope that leisure per se could extend to all workers positive compensation for the mediocrity of dull work in socially and technologically backward firms, indifferent to human factors.

However, even if this improvement in working conditions should be realized, one type of anxiety would persist. Analysis of relations between certain leisure activities and certain dynamic elements of working life has guided our study. To interpret, we have been forced to isolate work from the general social and cultural environment in which it is conducted. It was the only possible method. But prediction is neither dream nor prophecy. We must show, in conclusion, the limitations of our work. Are there not factors external to the work situation which may limit the effects of improvements which can be achieved in the latter? We fear particularly a useless and costly profusion of summary information and vulgar diversion sold by the great commercial mass media of communication. Could such a development not have, in the long run, destructive effects on the free social and cultural development of the masses? This question must not be evaded.

Finally, there is another source of anxiety. Despite the probable improvement in the condition of workers through the factors which we have analyzed, there will remain for a long period many individuals who will be condemned to be simple manual laborers without a stimulating social environment and without the opportunity for occupational promotion or union activity. How could they develop their participation in social responsibilities and cultural projects through leisure-time activity? This is one of the most serious questions for the immediate future of popular culture and for the long-run future of cultural values experienced by the masses.

To this question the results of our research provide no answer. They offer only a broad hypothesis which we expect to verify in research conducted in various economic, social, and political contexts.[46] In the firm of tomorrow, is it not possible that a portion of free time, thanks to the growth of productivity, might be invested in paid hours devoted to free apprenticeship and free self-improvement of employees? The education might be extended from work to activities off the job, in close relationship with schools, universities, and recreational and cultural associations. The modern firm would thus assume a cultural function which would prolong that of the school in a new manner. The 1960 World Congress of Adult Education (which included delegates from seventy nations) resolved that the era of education of mass society in the schools, opened toward the end of the nineteenth century, was coming to an end and that the new needs of our civilization call for a new era of permanent education which takes place throughout the life of children and adults. Is this not a possibility that is worthy of serious exploration if we wish to reduce these phenomena of maladjustment and sociocultural isolation which can make leisure as inhuman as work?

46. See comparative or actually coordinated research in progress in eight European countries: Germany (Federal Republic), Austria, Belgium, Finland, France, Poland, Switzerland, and Yugoslavia, under the auspices of the international group for the sociology of leisure and popular culture, created in 1956 at Amsterdam.

Suggestions for Additional Reading

Students who wish to probe further into the history of leisure will have to be resourceful. Material exists—indeed it exists in great quantities—but in a very scattered form. It is perhaps best to begin with some of the modern sociological literature, which can provide indications about historical developments, and can certainly raise some interesting questions. Bibliographical suggestions may be found in Reuel Denney and Mary Lea Meyersohn, "A Preliminary Bibliography on Leisure," in *The Uses of Leisure*, a special issue of the *American Journal of Sociology* 62 (1957): 602–615, reprinted in Wayne R. Williams, *Recreation Places* (New York: Reinhold, 1958), and also in Rolf Meyersohn, "A Comprehensive Bibliography on Leisure, 1900–1958," in *Mass Leisure*, eds. Eric Larrabee and Rolf Meyersohn (Glencoe, Ill.: The Free Press, 1958), pp. 389–419. The latter is an extremely useful collection of articles on the subject, as is Erwin O. Smigel, ed., *Work and Leisure: A Contemporary Social Problem* (New Haven, Conn.: College and University Press, 1963). On a related theme see the anthologies edited by Bernard Rosenberg and David Manning White, *Mass Culture: The Popular Arts in America* (New York: The Free Press, 1957) and *Mass Culture Revisited* (New York: Van Nostrand Reinhold, 1971), and the book by Russel Nye, *The Unembarrassed Muse: The Popular Arts in America* (New York: Dial Press, 1970), which has an excellent bibliography. Kenneth Roberts, *Leisure* (London: Longmans, 1970) is a competent, up-to-date survey, from a sociological point of view, and William R. Torbert, with Malcom P. Rogers, *Being for the Most Part Puppets: Interactions among Men's Labor, Leisure, and Politics* (Cambridge, Mass.: Schenkman, 1973) raises fascinating philosophical and psychological issues along with reporting on some current research. Students of European history may prefer to go first to two articles in *Past and Present:* Keith Thomas, "Work and Leisure in Pre-Industrial Society," 29 (1964): 50–62, with a following "Discussion," 63–66, and "Work and Leisure in Industrial Society: A Conference Report," 30 (1965): 96–103.

An extremely important theoretical work, originally published in 1944, is Johan Huizinga, *Homo Ludens: A Study of the Play Element in Culture* (Boston: Beacon Press, paperback edition, 1955). This work, along with Sebastian de Grazia's *Of Time, Work, and Leisure* (Garden City, N. Y.: Doubleday Anchor Books, 1964) will provide an excellent background to further study. Numerous investigations of European folklore are available, and these provide a special insight into the rhythms of popular life in traditional society —giving a necessary perspective for the study of modern forms of leisure. The best of these folkloric studies is probably Arnold Van Gennep's monumental *Manuel de folklore français contemporain,* 3 vols. (Paris: Editions Auguste Picard,

1937–1958) which has an almost inexhaustable store of information on the subject. The last two volumes of this work are bibliographies. Another excellent look at the fabric of popular life may be found in André Varagnac, *Civilisation traditionnelle et genres de vie* (Paris: Albin Michel, 1948).

But within this field of study a good deal of basic investigation must first be done before we will have reliable syntheses, and so students will find themselves quickly thrust upon their own resources. The best bibliographical tool for a study of the emergence of leisure is therefore the subject catalogue of any good library. With it students may pursue such themes as the development of spectator sports, vacations, dancing, drink, cinema, broadcasting, drama, advertising, popular literature, concerts, gambling, and so on.

In addition to the above suggestions the following books and articles may be noted as being of special interest:

Agulhon, Maurice. *Pénitents et Francs-Maçons de l'ancienne Provence.* Paris: Fayard, 1968.

―――. *La Vie sociale en Provence intérieure au lendemain de la Révolution.* Paris: Société des Études Robespierristes, 1970.

Brailsford, Dennis. *Sport and Society: Elizabeth to Anne.* Toronto: University of Toronto Press, 1969.

Briggs, Asa. *Mass Entertainment: The Origins of a Modern Industry.* The Joseph Fisher Lecture in Commerce. Adelaide, Australia, 1960.

Caillois, Roger. *Les Jeux et les hommes.* Paris: Gallimard, 1958.

Delgado, Alan. *Victorian Entertainment.* Newton Abbot, Eng.: David and Charles, 1971.

Dumazedier, Joffre. *Toward a Society of Leisure.* Translated by Stewart E. McClure. New York: The Free Press, 1967.

Geertz, Clifford. "Deep Play: Notes on the Balinese Cockfight." *Daedalus* (Winter 1972) pp. 1–37.

Giddens, A. "Notes on the Concepts of Play and Leisure."

Sociological Review 12 (1964): 73–89.

Harrison, Brian. *Drink and the Victorians: The Temperance Question in England, 1815–1872.* London: Faber and Faber, 1971.

————. "Religion and Recreation in Nineteenth-Century England." *Past and Present* 38 (1967): 98–125.

Heers, Jacques. *Fêtes, jeux, et joutes dans les sociétés d'Occident à la fin du Moyen Age.* Paris: Institute d'Etudes Médiévales, 1971.

Hoggart, Richard. *The Uses of Literacy: Aspects of Working-Class Life with Special Reference to Publications and Entertainments.* Harmondsworth, Eng.: Penguin, 1958.

Lowenthal, Leo. *Literature, Popular Culture, and Society.* Palo Alto, Calif.: Pacific Books, 1961.

McKechnie, Samuel. *Popular Entertainments through the Ages.* London: Sampson Low, Marston, 1931.

Mandrou, Robert. *De la culture populaire aux XVIIe et XVIIe siècles: la Bibliothèque bleue de Troyes.* Paris: Editions Stock, 1964.

Redlich, Fritz. "Leisure-Time Activities: A Historical, Sociological, and Economic Analysis." *Explorations in Entrepreneurial History* 3 (1965): 3–23.

Riesman, David. "Some Observations on Changes in Leisure Attitudes." in David Riesman, *Individualism Reconsidered and Other Essays.* Glencoe, Ill.: The Free Press, 1954.

Thompson, E. P. "Time, Work-Discipline, and Industrial Capitalism." *Past and Present* 38 (1967): 56–97.

Weber, Eugen. "Gymnastics and Sports in Fin-de-siècle France: Opium of the Classes?" *American Historical Review* 76 (1971): 70–98.

Wilson, Charles. "Economy and Society in Late Victorian Britain." *Economic History Review* 18 (1965) : 183–198.

74 75   12 11 10 9 8 7 6 5 4 3 2 1